Happy Birthday,

love from a

Marvin

5/9/82

Rosalind Rinker

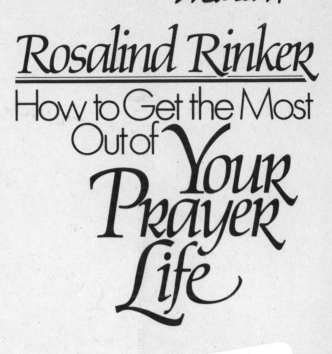

How to Get the Most Out of Your Prayer Life

HARVEST HOUSE PUBLISHERS
Eugene, Oregon 97402

Except where otherwise indicated, all Scripture quotations in this book are taken from the Revised Standard Version of the Bible, Copyright 1946 and 1952 by the Division of Christian Education of the National Council of the Churches of Christ in the United States of America. Used by permission.

HOW TO GET THE MOST OUT OF YOUR PRAYER LIFE

Copyright © 1981 by Rosalind Rinker
Published by Harvest House Publishers
Eugene, Oregon 97402

Library of Congress Catalog Card Number 81-81203
ISBN 0-89081-266-7

Printed in the United States of America.

CONTENTS

Books by Rosalind Rinker

1. The Years That Count
2. Prayer—Conversing With God
3. Who Is This Man?
4. You Can Witness With Confidence
5. The Open Heart
6. Communicating Love Through Prayer
7. Praying Together
8. Conversational Prayer
9. Within The Circle
10. Sharing God's Love
11. How To Have Family Prayers
12. Ask Me, Lord, I Want To Say Yes
13. Learning to Pray—Approaching God Through Creative Meditation
14. How To Get The Most Out Of Your Prayer Life

Preface

I never thought I'd be writing another book on prayer. Then one morning the telephone rang. Bob Hawkins on the line, a note of excitement in his voice: "I've got just the title for your next book. . . I wanted to call you last night when it came to me but my wife discouraged me. Here it is: *How to Get the Most Out of Your Prayer Life*. It would be a breeze for you, Ros, with all the hundreds of prayer workshops you've held the past few years, and God knows a book like this is needed."

Last year, when the issue of Crying Wind's books came up, Bob and I worked and prayed together, until it was possible to republish her books which have led so many to our Lord. Then one day he said, "Ros, why don't you do a book for me?" I laughed and replied, "After all these years why shouldn't I?" Then came the above telephone call.

I've known Bob Hawkins since my early days on staff when I was with Inter-Varsity (late 40s-late 50s). My territory covered four states: Oregon, Washington, Montana, and Idaho; and I covered those states in a Studebaker coupe. As I taught students, I learned the basics about practical, workable prayer, Bible study and personal evangelism. These became the subjects later for all my books.

I lived in Portland for seven years, and when student conferences were planned, I contacted a Christian bookstore that that (pardon, Bob) looked like a hole-in-the-wall but had a manager who was a real go-getter and promoter. Since then Bob has been engaged in a growing vocation, which included some years with Ken Taylor (Living Bibles) and seven years ago he founded his own publishing house, Harvest House. He says this book will be a winner. Why shouldn't I believe him!

I hope this book will be a winner for you, if you are one who picked it up because you want a better prayer-life. Prayer is a way of life, and I hope to develop that. I do my writing on the typewriter and the words and ideas just flow.

My thanks again to Bob Hawkins, and to Frances Forkish, my God-sent secretary and helper, and to all who listened and assisted me during the writing of this book.

Rosalind Rinker

Meditation for Chapter 1

Speak, Lord, in the stillness,
While I wait on Thee;
Hushed my heart to listen
In expectancy.

Speak, O blessed Master,
In this quiet hour;
Let me see Thy face, Lord,
Feel Thy touch of power.

For the words Thou speakest,
They are life indeed;
Living Bread from heaven,
Now my spirit feed!

All to Thee is yielded—
I am not my own;
Blissful, glad surrender—
I am Thine Alone.

Speak; Thy servant heareth!
Be not silent, Lord;
Waits my soul upon Thee
For the quick'ning word!
—E. May Grimes

CHAPTER 1

Stop Trying So Hard!

Do you remember *trying* to love someone?
Do you remember *falling* in love?

The first one, trying, sometimes defies effort, and the other just happens. Of course, falling in love means that you can *fall out of* love too. Trying to love means that there is some unsettled difficulty which stands between you and the other person.

God's love is different from human love in that He initiated it in the first place. He loved us before we ever were born, and He has loved us ever since, and He will love us forever. I believe that, and I hope you do too.

Why not relax and accept that great love? Learn to relax about your prayer time instead of wondering if you are going about it in the right way, or condemning yourself because you don't know what to do; and when you do know, you don't do it.

The Heart of Prayer

Prayer is a language between two people who love each other. Prayer is the love-language of the heart.

The heart of prayer is the never-changing truth that God loves you unconditionally, regardless of who you are or what you have done or have not done. This truth should draw from your heart and mine a response of total commitment made with joy and thankfulness.

You and I forget how much we are loved and how near our Lord Jesus always is to us, and the result is guilt, condemnation, and then depression. Affirmations can help us make this truth our own.

Affirmations

An affirmation is a positive statement of truth, which, when constantly repeated, sinks into the subconscious and becomes part of us. By constant repetition I mean something like 100 times a day. Try these—they brought self-acceptance to me.

Say them to yourself, say them aloud, and soon you will be telling someone else.

An Exercise in Love

I am loved.
I am loved unconditionally—not on a merit basis.
I am loved because God made me for His own.

— — — —

You are loved.
You are loved unconditionally—not on a merit basis.
You are loved. Period.
You are loved because God is love, and because He told us so in His Word.

Relax and Let God Love You

"Let God love you" is a phrase often used by Lloyd J. Ogilvie, pastor of Hollywood Presbyterian Church. He has written a book by that name.

Love does not find it difficult to make time for being with a loved one, nor to express one's most intimate thoughts. Everything can be poured out, knowing that the loved one is listening and will sort it all out and understand, and will love you just the same.

This is what prayer does.

This is what prayer means.

Our Father in heaven sorts out everything, and more than that, He knows everything. Miracle of miracles, He accepts you and me just as we are!

So relax. Accept the truth that *you are loved*, and give the Lord our God the love of your heart, mind, body, and soul.

Knowing and accepting the fact that you are loved unconditionally and forgiven freely should mean that you come into His presence just as you are.

You are loved.

You are accepted.

He will teach the teachable by His Spirit.

Now Make a Few Decisions

1. Since prayer (talking to and with your Lord) is the key to your spiritual growth, decide that you will have a daily, regular time to meet Him.

2. Before I go to bed at night, I ask the Lord to awaken me in the morning, ready to meet Him, and ready to get up.

3. I awaken with, "Thank You, Lord God, Thank You, Lord Jesus, for the night's rest.

Thank You for the day ahead."

4. Decide to get up immediately, wash, and slip into something comfortable.

5. Find a solitary place where you can be alone. This isn't always easy, but you can find a place if you will ask the Lord to help you find one wherever you are.

Here are a few of the "morning places" I've found in my long pilgrimage where I've kept tryst with Jesus.

by a certain place at my bedside on my
  knees
in a certain chair facing the window
up in an attic facing the west window
in my car where I can see trees or water
in a room with four other people, facing
  the wall
at the kitchen table
on the back porch facing a mountain
on a cliff overlooking the ocean

6. This is time alone with my God, so I find a place where I'm not facing people (close up, that is.)

Start with ten minutes.
Keep the time definite.
Increase the time as desired.

Let's quickly review those six points so they stick.

1. Make the decision.
2. Pray to be awakened.
3. Wake up giving thanks.
4. Get up immediately.
5. Find a solitary place.
6. Start with ten minutes.

The hard part is making the decision; after

that it's easy. Then comes the little routine which will very quickly mean a great deal to you, such as what to say to God, how much to pray, how much to read, what exactly to read in your Bible. The later chapters will give more simple, effective suggestions from which you may select.

The important part is that you are having a tryst with the One who loves you the most in all this world, who has a plan for your life, and who can always be trusted to do the most loving things.

Your Helper

The gift of the Holy Spirit is given to all believers that they may have a Teacher and a Guide. Trust this Helper, this Comforter, and you'll see how easy it is to stop trying and to just follow, to just listen (John 14:16-18, 26).

My Next Experiences

It was after I went to China in my 20's as a missionary that I learned how to spend longer times in prayer.

I'll never forget those days, and what they meant to me in getting close to my beloved Lord. I was leading a team of four Chinese girls from our seminary on a certain trip into the rural villages of China, where conditions were quite primitive compared to the way we live in the city.

Often the only way I could be alone with the Lord was to sit cross-legged facing the wall and ignoring the four girls. Very soon they were doing the same thing, and so we all had our daily morning Quiet Time.

But that wasn't enough, it seems, for we were in the enemy's territory, where the name of Jesus had not been heard. The Light was coming into the darkness.

In Him was life, and the life was the light of men. The light shines in the darkness, and the darkness has not overcome it (John 1:4,5).

The true light that enlightens every man was coming into the world (John 1:9).

Light casting out darkness can mean conflict.

The inner calling to pray was so strong that I began to look for a place to pray.

Then I prayed for a place to pray, remembering that I have a Helper to guide and direct me. I was very definitely led to the little bare-earth chapel, with sawhorses (no back) for seats. It was empty when no meetings were being held.

This was the place! But that cold, damp floor? Well, I wore a padded *cheung sham*, which was long and warm, and I had sheepskin-lined short boots. I looked around, and there it was! Just the thing! A pile of straw mats which the Christians used to kneel on when the service was in progress. A few of them piled together did the trick.

For the first time in my life I wanted to be alone in prayer for a long, long time . . . yes, even hours. I desired with a great longing desire to be on my knees and to pour out my heart for all the desperation, ignorance, and darkness around me. Also, my heart needed the touch of God's Spirit to renew and empower me with His holy presence.

There were times when many words came, sometimes in English and sometimes in Chinese. Then there would be no words at all, and then tears, and then silence that spoke louder than words.

There was power then to cast out the enemy, whose territory we had invaded, and as a team we had unity, love, and freedom to give the gospel to people who wanted to hear. Those whose ears were opened to hear (Matthew 13:9) became believers, and learned of God's love for them.

Another Kind of Prayer

I was in my late 20's and early 30's in those days. When the Japanese war broke out in China I had just gone home on furlough, and so escaped the concentration camps. At that time I finished my college work, receiving a B.A. from Asbury College, in Kentucky. Immediately I applied and was accepted as a staff member by Inter-Varsity Christian Fellowship for the Pacific Northwest states. Driving that little Studebaker over all that vast territory, I learned another kind of prayer—prayer at the wheel!

I sometimes smile to myself when a driver I'm with brings her car to a complete stop, closes her eyes, and prays for a safe trip.

Pray with your eyes open!

Pray anywhere—driving, walking, working.

Thank you, Lord Jesus, for being right here with me, in this car. Restrain the other drivers, and give me quick reactions.

Then I continue to talk to Him about where I'm going and what I'm doing. I give thanks continually for all the growing, green things my eyes can see.

Prayer is a conversation with someone you love.

How to Handle Condemnation

Do you still feel guilty and condemn yourself because you do not keep a daily, regular Quiet Time for devotions? I hope by this time you have asked forgiveness for both your irregularity and your allowing condemnation to stay with you. Stop. Do it now in a short sentence or two. Simply putting your feelings into words brings release.

I remember vividly the first time I decided to tell on myself, to admit to others that my Q.T. was irregular or neglected, and how I handled it. I was teaching a class of students at summer camp on Catalina Island (IVCF) at the time. After I told them, there was a startled silence, and then questions began to come from all sides. But great gratitude and relief that one of their staff members would admit failure and share it with them allowed them to begin to handle their own failure in this area.

What's the secret of living with my human self and its ups and downs, even in my devotional life? That I am loved by God, that through His Holy Spirit, Jesus Christ is always *within me* and *with me*. I am never alone. I've learned to carry on an almost-endless conversation with Him all day long, about everything and anything.

Remember to tell yourself:

God loves me.

God accepts me just as I am.

I am loved by God.

Stop trying so hard and let God love you!

The love of God (Father, Son, and Holy Spirit) will remind you, will nudge you, will draw you to Himself until you gladly, once more and afresh, make time for Him.

Review

Group Sharing

1. Define and illustrate an affirmation. What is its purpose?

2. List the affirmations given, and put them where you can see them for a few days. Practice them.

3. Share with each other your Quiet Time (devotional) habits and problems.

4. Does God's love depend on my faithfulness? Why not?

Group Activity

1. Stand in a circle, holding hands, and pray short, specific sentence prayers for each other.

2. Close by using the meditation printed at the beginning of this chapter in various ways as you are led.

Meditation for Chapter 2

I am the Lord's! O joy beyond expression,
O sweet response to voice of love divine;
Faith's joyous "Yes" to the assuring whisper,
"Fear not! I have redeemed thee; thou art
Mine."

I am the Lord's! Yes, body, soul, and spirit;
O seal them irrecoverably Thine,
As Thou, Beloved, in Thy grace and fulness
Forever and forevermore art mine.

—Lucy A. Bennett

CHAPTER 2

You Can Know Who You Are

Do you know who *you* are?

If you read the first chapter (some people do skip around) there is one great truth which was repeated over and over; you will know one thing for sure: You are loved.

You, a unique person, are loved by God.

What a wonderful thing it is to be loved by God!

What a freedom, what a treasure to explore, what a way to start each new day!

Do you *know* who you are?

An Honest Answer

Were you ever in a group where you were asked to quietly think who you are, then write it and share it? That can be a shattering, even a life-changing experience, for an honest disclosure helps remove the mask. It reveals you, the innermost you, the part of you that cares and loves. Then next on the program comes acceptance by a loving support-group. Here is what one honest woman wrote and shared:

> I am a middle-aged woman, a widow, who is continually pulling on her 12-year-old son for the love and understanding denied to her by life. I need help.

How honest can one be!

What would *you* write down?

How long do you think it would take you to

be willing not only to write it but to share it? You must be aware that all of us are different persons at different stages of our lives. I'm talking about right now.

Knowing who you really are is one of the important keys on the ring of how to make your prayer life more satisfactory. This is because prayer links you closely to the One who knows you and who can tell you who you are.

Assignment for Right Now

On a piece of paper, in a few short sentences, tell yourself who you really are. Keep that paper in your Bible and review it in a day or two. Keep talking to Jesus about yourself, and keep your heart open. He knew who He was, who He is, and who He will be forever. He loves you and He has plans for you.

Support-Group

In a support-group there are partners who pray together. If you don't have one, well . . . I count, don't I? If it helps, you can write me (care of the publisher) and I'll pray for you and support you.

You'll want to know who I, Ros Rinker, am. Right now, today, I know who I am. That hasn't always been true, and I have prayer-partners to thank for their support.

This Is Who I Am

I am a 75-year-old single woman who always wanted to be married and who still lives alone.

However—

I am a child of God and I know it.

I am loved by God and I know it.

I am in the will and plan of God and I know it.

Jesus Christ my Lord, by His love and presence, has poured a fountain of living water into my heart which fulfills all my needs. Daily I drink deeply (John 4:10-14; 7:37-39).

With Mary, the Virgin Mother, I praise my Lord: He who is mighty has done great things for me! My spirit (heart and body) rejoices! He has filled the hungry with good things. Holy is His Name. (See Luke 1:46-55.)

Father/Child Relationship

Being a member of the human race, each one of us has a father, whether we know him or not. Being a member of God's family, we have a heavenly father, and we need to know Him, as well as ourselves.

Question: Which comes first—knowing that God loves me, or knowing that I am His child?

Answer: That depends on your receptivity, your knowledge of Him, and perhaps the circumstances which bring the good news to you.

Question: I hope I'm a child of God. I want to be His child, but so many times I'm not sure.

Answer: It is a vital step to a fulfilled prayer life. I can see your problem, which is that you are confusing *relationship*

My question: (being God's child) with *fellowship* (which is daily living and all the problems it brings). Let me ask you a question. When is your birthday? No problem. When is your *spiritual* birthday? A problem?

Relationship naturally precedes fellowship. This is true in a family when a child is born; the birthdate is recorded. This is also true of a marriage, in which a new relationship begins. This is also true of our Father/child relationship with our Lord. We know when it happened. We were there.

My Relationships

My physical birthdate is April 2, 1906, in New Rockford, North Dakota.

My spiritual birthdate is June 25, 1921. It happened in Jamestown, North Dakota, at an old-fashioned camp meeting where my mother took me when I was 15 years old.

I was there when it happened. I heard people talk about Jesus Christ in a tone of voice I had never heard before. I saw a light on their faces when they talked about Him that made me hungry to know Him like that too. So when an invitation was given, I was ready and went forward and knelt at an altar of prayer. I had no sooner knelt there than a great light shone all around me, and I sprang to my knees, wanting to sing, to praise God, to give expression to that light and joy within me.

After that, fellowship began: It was easy to

pray, my Bible made sense, and I wanted to be with others who belonged to Jesus by relationship—not by hearsay, nor by church membership, nor by head-belief (which was my previous status).

Your Relationship

Your relationship can begin at any moment in time when you give your consent. I'm sure you've seen Billy Graham campaign invitations, and know all about what goes on.

If your heart is open and longing *to know for sure*, that's a good sign. Get your Bible, and turn to John 6:44: "No one can come to me unless the Father who sent me draws him; and I will raise him up at the last day."

There are beautiful truths in that verse.

1. The desire in your heart is placed there by God.

2. You are being drawn, like a magnet draws steel.

3. In His presence now, acknowledge this to be true.

4. You are to be His forever, now and forever.

As a strong basis for your faith, you must understand that you are putting your trust, yourself, in a *Person*, Jesus Christ—not in a church, or a denomination, or any form of theology.

> He himself bore our sins in his body on the tree, that we might die to sin and live to righteousness. By his wounds you have been healed. For you were straying like sheep, but have now

returned to the Shepherd and Guardian of your souls (1 Peter 2:24,25).

1. Read it. Then read it aloud until you get the meaning.

2. Now substitute *I* for *we*, *me* for *you*. This makes it personal; it means *you*. Read it aloud.

3. Invite the Lord Jesus into your heart, if you have never done so. If you have done so but still aren't sure, tell Him you believe these verses. Tell Him, "I believe it is a gift, and not anything I can earn, and I give thanks to You that I am Your child by faith in You. Thank You for taking all my sins, for which I sincerely and humbly am sorry. Thank You, Lord Jesus."

4. Doubts again, or later? Give thanks, over and over. Thanksgiving is a miracle-way to pray. It works for everybody I know, and it will work for you. How do you take care of failure and guilt? More about this later.

5. Then for joy, share it with someone.

6. Now turn to the three letters of John near the back of your New Testament, and read them. Reread them, and underline what speaks to you. You could even write today's date in the margin as a monument to remember.

Which Comes First?

We are back to that first question: Does relationship come first or knowledge of God's love come first?

If I were following my early life-history, I might say that relationship came first. I had knowledge, the kind that comes from church attendance, but I did not have Life with a

capital L. I did not know I was God's child.
Jesus was only a historical Person—not a real
Personage who could live in my heart.

Thank God, He works with us in any way
and at any time He can, to draw us to Himself
regardless of what we know or don't know.

The drawing power of love is the greatest
power in the world. Read the following
sentences aloud. There's no question which
has the attraction that gets your attention.

1. God loves you and
accepts you as you are.

2. You are a sinner and
need to be born again.

Both of them are true, but the first one gives
a person hope. And hope is the mother of
faith. And faith comes by hearing. The second
statement is one of fact, and as it stands it gives
no hope at all.

But who can compete against unconditional
eternal love, in the way God our Father revealed Himself to the world through His Son,
Jesus Christ our Lord!

What in all of God's universe can separate
me from His love? Romans 8:31-39 gives a most
comprehensive list of things that cannot
separate me from His love, but in spite of this I
had the effronty and ignorance to say, "Yes,
but my own sin can." Little did I realize at that
time what I was doing. I was making any sin
that I might be overtaken in greater than God
Himself and Christ's atonement on the cross.

We have a Great High Priest who once for all

became a sin offering. Never again does He have to come and die for the sins of mankind (Hebrews 9:24-26).

I came to the final and firm conclusion that, because of Jesus Christ, God loves and accepts me just as I am. Because I am His child, He does correct and discipline me, and guide me into His ways. What absolute peace! What security! What rest of spirit!

Can Relationship Be Broken?

Yes, human relationships can be broken—by death, distance, estrangement, etc. But there always seems to remain a part of those persons present with us.

Relationship with God and His child is an eternal transaction. Once His child, always His child. True or false? Churches have divided over this, and theology exists for both sides. I've been on both sides of that fence.

Now read the words of Jesus Christ:

I am the resurrection, and life; he who believes in me, though he die, yet shall he live, and whoever lives and believes in me shall never die. Do you believe this? (John 11:25,26).

My sheep hear my voice, and I know them, and they follow me; and I give them eternal life, and they shall never perish, and no one shall snatch them out of my hand. My Father, who has given them to me, is greater than all, and no one is able to snatch them out of

the Father's hand. I and the Father are
one (John 10:27-30).

Question: What does knowing who you are
have to do with an effectual prayer
life? Isn't it more important to learn
to pray and get answers? To pray for
miracles and get answers? To pray
for healings and get answers?

Answer: Let's go back to the human relationship again: How can I ask someone
to whom I'm not related to do a very
personal favor for me?

The first step in prayer is knowing that God
loves you and that He loves every person
whom He has put on this earth. The result of
that love will soon be a relationship, and you'll
know for sure that you are God's child.

Then, as a member of His family, as a beloved member who has access to your Father,
you are assured that at all times He is available.

Can Fellowship Be Broken?

Yes, fellowship on earth can be broken, for it
is dependent on many things, such as my
cooperation in seeking His face and in being
obedient to His will. However, I cannot really
end a relationship; I can only break it off and
avoid that person.

I can break my fellowship with God by
avoiding His will, by not listening to His voice,
by going my own way instead of His. That is
what sin is, and when we sin, immediate confession restores the fellowship (1 John 1:7-9).

Moreover, the life, death, and resurrection of

Jesus Christ ensures the relationship (Romans 5:10).

An Exercise in Love

Tell someone today, "God loves you." If you ask (pray) for an opportunity to do this, it will be there.

Ask someone today, "Do you know how very much God loves you?" To ask, in this case, is like telling.

Perhaps you should stop and tell this to yourself first, over and over. Affirm it all day long. Before you realize what is happening, you'll be telling someone else, and God knows we all need to hear it over and over.

This is the message:

God loves you.

You are loved by God.

You can know you are His child.

P.S. God's love is not based on some good or kind thing you did, nor does He remove His love when we do bad things (sin). That is because His love is based on His very own Person:

I am the Lord Jehovah.

I change not.

I have loved you with everlasting love (Romans 8:26-39; Jeremiah 31:3).

Review

Group Sharing

1. Which came first with you—relationship

with God, or knowing that He loves you?

2. Discuss the difference between relationship and fellowship.

3. What breaks fellowship and what restores it?

4. Do you know who you are? Write it out.

Group Activity

1. Tell everyone now (in your group) that *God loves you*. (It's like "passing the peace" with arms!)

2. Before you go to bed tonight, tell each member of your family at the right time, *"God loves you and I love you too."*

3. Tell this to five other people you meet anywhere.

4. The next time you meet with the group, report what happened.

5. Close by using the meditation printed at the beginning of this chapter in various ways as you are led.

Meditation for Chapter 3

Sing them over again to me,
   Wonderful words of life;
Let me more of their beauty see,
   Wonderful words of life;
Words of life and beauty,
   Teach me faith and duty:
Beautiful words, wonderful words,
   Wonderful words of Life.

           —Philip P. Bliss

CHAPTER 3

How to Pray-Read
Your Bible

To pray-read means to pray and read your Bible at the same time.[1] In other words, when you read and pray, ask yourself:

Is there a promise for me to claim today?

Is there a command that I should follow?

Is there a sin for me to confess?

Is there something to give thanks or praise for?

The whole Bible is about our Lord, the Redeemer and Saviour of mankind. Both Old and New Testaments tell about Him.

The New is in the Old contained, and the Old is by the New explained.

Four Basic Steps in Prayer

These steps can be used anywhere, anytime, alone or with a group. I'd like to have you begin to use them in your pray-reading time. They have become second nature to me now, and it doesn't matter which step comes first. I talk with Jesus when I'm driving, swimming, or walking—all day long with open-ended prayer —that is, not closing by saying "Amen."

---

[1]The Catholics have a whole series of small booklets on how to read and pray the Bible. May be obtained by writing S.C.R.C., P.O. Box 45594, Los Angeles, CA 90045.

One young man, after getting hold of these four basic steps, came back after driving a truck all day to report, "Ros, those four steps really work. I didn't know how to pray before." He was encouraged because he could say simple words and broken sentences, and pray from his heart to Jesus, who is with him.

1. Worship: *Jesus is here* (Matthew 18:18-20).
2. Thanksgiving: *Thank You, Lord (for . . .)* (Philippians 4:4-7).
3. Confession: *Forgive me, Lord (for . . .)* (1 John 1:9).
4. Intercession: *Help my brother/sister (to . . .)* (Mark 11:22-25).[2]

Stop a moment and memorize those four key words—two about our Lord, one about me, and one about someone I'm praying for.

Now look at the short prayer after each key word. How many words are in these prayers? When you know those three of four words and the short prayers that go with them, you are on your way to real praying. You can add to each one anything you wish, and it will be different every time.

That's because the Holy Spirit is given to us to be our Teacher and Helper and to pray through us when we don't know what to say except Jesus' name and the friend's name.

---

[2]Short pamphlet with further instruction: *Aids to Conversation Prayer*, Dove Publications, Pecos, New Mexico 87552.

Two Things to Remember

Two things will make prayer a living force and power in your life:

1. Pray to Jesus.
2. Pray from the child in your heart.

You can pray to the Father and to the Holy Spirit also, but it helps to find out as you read your Bible just what each member of the Trinity does, so you can pray with more faith. More on this later.

The Child in Your Heart

Pray to Jesus from the child in your heart.

Everyone has a child within, a child that needs love, understanding, and holding-arms. Read Mark 10:13-16 and see how Jesus taught His disciples to become like children, and how He loved them.

Being a child means being childlike, open, and honest, and not using flowery adult phrases or Thee's and Thou's. It just means talking to Jesus, who loves you, and listening to what He has to say to you. Listening is a big part of prayer too.

Prayer is a language of the heart, and that is the best way to just say what your heart is saying.

Since I have five books on the subject of prayer,[3] I won't enlarge on the simple dynamics of conversational prayer here. The

[3]*Prayer-Conversing with God, Communicating Love Through Prayer, Conversational Prayer, Praying Together,* and *How to Have Family Prayers.*

first book, *Prayer-Conversing With God* (Zondervan), is now a best-seller, translated into nine languages.[4]

How to Read Your Bible

When I started to write this chapter, it went pretty slowly until I realized that I had to preface it with a little talk on "praying to Jesus from your heart" because this is one of the secrets of understanding your Bible.

I'll tell you another secret—the secret of spiritual growth, which is being fed properly. What milk is to the newborn baby, so is the Word of God to newborn believers and to all believers. Do you want to grow spiritually? Do you want a better prayer life? Learn how to read your Bible, for it is there that God speaks to you. It will become the source of wisdom and guidance, of comfort and blessing, to which you will return daily for the problems that life hands you.

There are many ways to read your Bible, and you'll find (like I did) that you want to change and use another way every few years in order to stimulate your thinking and interest.

1. *Topical study, by word or subject*
Teenagers like this kind of study. For instance, take the word *love* or *faith* or any word you like, and look it up in your concordance. Some Bibles have short concordances in the back. If yours doesn't, buy a good one for

[4]Afrikaans, Chinese, Dutch, Finnish, Indonesian, Japanese, Korean, Spanish, Swedish.

yourself at a Christian bookstore; you'll use it all your life. Keep a notebook and write what you find; study and compare, and you'll learn a lot.

2. *Reading through a Gospel*

It is important that you know one Gospel well. Take the Gospel of John and read a chapter a day, either morning or evening. It has 21 chapters, so you could even skip a day or two and still read it through in less than a month.

Then turn right around and read it again. Do this for six months, and sometimes use a different translation of the Bible (see list Review #4) until you know which chapters are your favorites, which chapters seem to speak to you the most.

Use a card or small ruler for underlining, so that your lines are straight. (Otherwise the pages soon look messy.)

Here is a brief summary of the Gospels.

Matthew: written for Jewish believers; has many Old Testament references.

Mark: written for Greek believers; very few teaching passages; lots of action.

Luke: written by the physician Luke, with facts, historical personages, and many teaching passages.

John: written to show the deity of our Lord; teaching passages based on specific subjects or miracles; in-depth devotional chapters.

3. *Making the Psalms your own prayer book*

Some Psalms are prayers all the way through, using "I" and "me," and it is easy to make them your own. Pray along with David for yourself by repeating them and adding your own words.

Turn to Psalm 32, and follow these verses:

a) statement of fact (v. 1): "Blessed is he whose . . ."

b) prayer (v. 5): "I acknowledged my sin to thee . . ."

c) God speaking (v. 8): "I will instruct you and teach you the way you should go; I will counsel you with my eye upon you."

One problem in the Psalms—when David asks that terrible things happen to his enemies. Remember that this is the Old Testament principle of "an eye for an eye" and that we are now living in New Testament truth: Jesus taught us to pray for our enemies. When I read these "imprecatory" prayers, I make "the enemy" that nature of sin within me that wants to go my own way, that hurts others, that disobeys God.

4. *In-depth study for advanced students*

Three questions get to the heart of the passage, put meaning before application, and are used in *inductive* study:

a) What does this passage say
(to those to whom it was written)?

b) What does it mean (now)?

c) What does it mean to me?

I didn't start in-depth studies until at least 20 years after my conversion. As my guides I used booklets like the ones following.

Bible Study Booklets with Daily Readings

1. *This Morning With God*, Volumes I, II, III, IV, InterVarsity Press, Downers Grove, Illinois 60615. Each volume has some books from the Old Testament and some from the New Testament, with a paragraph of notes daily, taking you through the Bible in five years. The inductive method is used: contrast and comparison, repetition of words and ideas, asking how, what, where, and when.
2. *Bible Reading Fellowship* (BRF), P.O. Box M, Winter Park, Florida 32790. An Episcopal publication with small, bimonthly booklets. Send for samples.
   Series A. Senior study notes on Bible passages.
   Series B. Brief daily notes with Bible passages printed in full.
   Compass. Illustrated workbook for children.
3. Scripture Union, 1716 Spruce Street, Philadelphia, Pennsylvania 19103. A similar set (as above) for various ages, originally from England, and also a reliable source.

Devotional Books

These include books with daily readings

based on a verse of Scripture. This does not take the place of getting the Bible into your own hands and reading it prayerfully and thoughtfully. However, books like these abound in Christian bookstores, and everyone has favorites.

There are two of these which helped me the most, and I read them for almost 20 years: *My Utmost for His Highest,* by Oswald Chambers (for challenge and truth), and *Streams in the Desert,* by Mrs. Charles Cowman (for comfort and blessing).

Then there are the various monthly or bi-monthly pocket-sized daily reading books which almost every denomination puts out.

God Will Speak to You

God is speaking all the time, all the time, all the time, Frank Laubach once told me. It is my business to listen and be alert to His voice. He speaks to us through circumstances, through our friends, and through the Bible.

The Holy Spirit is given to be our Teacher, so Psalm 119:18 is a good verse to use as an opening prayer:

Open my eyes, that I may behold
wondrous things out of thy law.

I remember a young Chinese student expressing it like this: "Why, those Chinese characters [words] just seem to stand up on their feet and speak to me as if they had voices. I *know* they are talking to me." That made a lasting impression on me as a young missionary.

No matter how you read your Bible, the still, small voice of the Lord will speak to you. You will find that you need some kind of guide or plan, or else days will get too busy and you will miss out.

"How do I know when God speaks to me?" is the question I'm often asked. When is it my own thoughts, and when isn't it? I have a test: If it is a loving thought, I am delighted. If it is a difficult thought which I'm holding back on, I pray, "Lord, if You are talking to me, just keep on, because I want to hear; but if that isn't Your voice, let those thoughts fall to the ground like water, which can't be picked up again." That works fine for me.

Review

Group Sharing

1. How many ways are listed in this chapter to study your Bible? Make a list to remind you.
2. Which ways have you used, and which ways would you like to start using?
3. Discuss the translations of the Bible you own and why you like them.
4. Consider the following translations of the Bible:
    For general use: New American Standard Bible, Revised Standard Version, or New International Version.
    For traditional use: King James Version or

New King James Version. (The New KJV is quite readable.)

For rapid reading (paraphrases): The Living Bible, the Good News Bible, or the New Testament in Modern English (Phillips).

For further comparisons: Amplified Bible, New Berkeley Version, New English Bible, or New American Bible.

Group Activity

1. Pray-read Psalm 32 together.
   a) Read it silently first.
   b) Then read it aloud from one or more versions.
   c) Each person pray-read a verse, in simple sentences as they come to you with your eyes open upon the verse.
2. Close by using the meditation printed at the beginning of this chapter in various ways as you are led.

Meditation for Chapter 4

Fairest Lord Jesus, Ruler of all nature,
O Thou of God and man the Son,
Thee will I cherish, Thee will I honor,
Thou my soul's glory, joy, and crown.

All fairest beauty, heavenly and earthly,
Wondrously, Jesus, is found in Thee;
None can be nearer, fairer, or dearer,
Than Thou my Savior art to me.

—From *Munster Gesangbuch*

CHAPTER 4

How to Practice the Presence of God

The title of this chapter is a familiar one to many of us, since it reminds us of Brother Lawrence's old but famous *Practise of the Presence of God.*

The message is this: God is always with you. Call Him to mind often, and make Him part of your everyday life. Live your whole life in His presence.

I remember the longing in my heart as a teenager when I read an old copy of that little pamphlet. I wanted Jesus to be that real to me also. Right from the moment of my conversion, at age 15, I have been a Christ-centered believer; God the Father and God the Holy Spirit have since become real to me also. I believe that it is the privilege of every believer to have a personal experience with each member of our triune God.

Brother Lawrence was a medieval monk whose duty was to scrub the uneven brick floors of the monastery kitchen and to wash the huge kettles in which food had been prepared. It was not a very spiritual-sounding job, but he looked upon it as a way to give praise and thanks to his Lord, who suffered on the cross for him. He scrubbed floors on his knees to the glory of God, and he kept a running praise-and-prayer dialogue in his heart no matter how unpleasant or tiring the job.

We had a modern-age Brother Lawrence in our midst for a few years, who has now gone to be with his Lord. His name was Frank Laubach, better known to many people as the man who initiated the each-one-teach-one method of reading as a means of coping with illiteracy. I knew him as a person with a great heart of love for the world and for all people, as we shared the platform in several Camps Farthest Out in the Midwest in the 60's. I immediately bought and devoured all his books.

I remember an incident which happened one afternoon as some of us were sitting together. Someone asked me where I got the liberty and authority to speak as I did. I sat there silently, not knowing how to answer, and Brother Frank answered for me.

"The price of that kind of liberty and authority is suffering," he said with that quiet, wise way he had about him.

He also taught me something else which only could have been prompted by the Holy Spirit. We were at a dinner table with eight or ten others, and he looked across at me and asked, "Would you like to know how I take a walk? I use my walking time as my prayer time also. Everything my eyes see I give thanks for: every different kind of leaf, flower, bird, color—the sky, the clouds, the wind . . . whatever has been made by the hand of my Creator. I give thanks and glory to Him in short sentences of praise."

At once that kind of walking-praise became a practice of mine. I still do it even when I'm driving alone in my car.

Then I got my hands on an early booklet he wrote as a young missionary to the Philippine Islands. He felt so alone in the great task before him and the darkness of the people around him that he started writing down his daily thoughts and prayers. Then came the little booklet that in the minds of many has taken its place beside the teaching of Brother Lawrence.

It is titled *The Game of Minutes.* Frank firmly believed that offering the sacrifice of praise, whether one felt like it nor not (Psalm 50:23) was a weapon to defeat our common enemy, a way to open the gates of heaven for answered prayer, and a way to remind ourselves of God's presence always with us. He showed us how to do it all day long by developing a habit which anyone can do, and he called it *The Game of Minutes.*

Briefly, every hour on the hour, one remembers to offer praise or thanks to the Lord God in short, heartfelt sentences. Like:

Praise to you, Lord Christ.

Praise, honor, and glory to you, Lord Jesus.

Thank you, Father, for this beautiful earth.

Thank you, Father, for the gift of Your Son.

Jesus, I love you.

Any one of those, or others which come to your mind, offer to Jesus with the deep thanksgiving and adoration of your whole being.

Living in His presence

Such hourly devotion and praise is known as "practicing the presence of God" or "living in His presence."

If you start to search the Bible for evidence of this kind of "living with God" it will take you back to the Old Testament. Jehovah revealed Himself to Moses in the burning bush, and He promised to be with him all the way. In the desert wilderness, Jehovah accompanied the children of Israel:

> And the Lord went before them by day in a pillar of cloud to lead them the way, and by night in a pillar of fire to give them light, to go by day and night. He took not away the pillar of the cloud by day nor the pillar of fire by night from before the people.
>
> (Exodus 13:21,22 KJV).

Such evidences of God's presence with His people were not everyday occurences. They happened only on special occasions, as to David, a man after His own heart, or to the prophets, to whom "the Word of the Lord came" in instruction, rebuke and comfort.

Then the New Testament era began with a "voice in the wilderness" as John the Baptist announced the coming One who would forgive people's sins and baptize them with the Holy Spirit.

Jehovah-God came to earth in the Person of

His Son, Jesus, who assured us by His example and His teaching that He and His Father love us and want to live within us, as the branch lives within the vine (John 15). In His high-priestly prayer for all His disciples, Jesus assures us that we are one and are loved "just as the Father" loved Him, and He implies that this love would enable us to love one another in the same way.

Very plainly we have the truth of God living within each one of us—loving us, protecting us from evil, guiding us, and communicating with us.

Then, after Jesus' resurrection, this was brought about by the Holy Spirit coming upon all His disciples gathered in the upper room. Jesus taught them before He left them, "I will never leave you nor forsake you." "Lo, I am with you always, even to the end of the world."

Paul in Galatians 2:20 affirms this same presence within us: "It is no longer I who live, but Christ who lives in me; and the life I now live in the flesh I live by faith in the Son of God, who loved me and gave himself for me."

No longer only revealing Himself to certain chosen ones on certain occasions, our Lord God now desires to live within each person who invites Him in, and He communicates with us in various ways, but He does need our cooperation.

This is where the *Game of Minutes* comes in—to remind and discipline our busy and sometimes neglectful minds.

Monthly I receive a newsletter from the

Benedictine Abbey in Pecos, New Mexico, which prints in full the new leaflets they are adding to their already-long list. They print my "Aids to Conversational Prayer," and that is how I know about them. In the April 1981 newsletter they have a new pamphlet titled *Living in His Presence*, by Fr. Andrew Miles, O.S.B.

I read it after I had written a few pages of this chapter, and that stopped me cold. How much better Fr. Andrew had stated the whole case of "living in the presence of God" every day than I could possibly do! I left my typewriter and went to my usual Friday morning prayer meeting. By the time I got around to writing again, I was assured by the Lord, who is always with me, that I would receive His help also, and that Fr. Andrew couldn't have done it either without help from the Spirit of God.

I am going to list the areas of our lives which he has mentioned that we can share with our Lord, as we remember His presence with us.

1. Share every part of your work.
2. All your relationships will be enriched.
3. Share your leisure time, such as walking or jogging.
4. At mealtimes invite Him to be your guest.
5. Remember Him before you go to sleep, and when you awake.
6. Every aspect of your person can be used to experience His presence. Here is a brief summary of how to give the Lord your total self:

eyes: to see beauty, to share compassion.
ears: to hear sounds we are too busy to hear.
feelings and emotions: bring them to Him.
mind: to think His positive, loving thoughts.
wills: daily, repeatedly surrendered to Him.
heart: with its affections and love.

In his leaflet,[1] Fr. Andrew quotes directly from Brother Lawrence: "Perseverance is required in making a habit of conversing with God and of referring all we do to him, but after a little His love moves us to do it without any difficulty."

Helps to Remind Us

Both Brother Frank and Fr. Andrew suggest the use of various articles in your home or your study to remind you to give a word of praise or thanks every hour on the hour. This is not an easy habit to acquire, and at first you'll forget many times; when you do, simply ask God to forgive you and to remind you when the next hour comes.

Objects placed around your room, home, or study will help, such as an open Bible, a picture of Jesus (I like the one with the children around Him), a cross or crucifix, a chiming clock, a Bible verse framed. Look around your

---

[1]This is available in full from Dove Publications, Pecos, New Mexico 87552.

room now and see what is already there to remind you of your Lord.

Making a habit of thanking the Lord at all
times for all things, good or bad, pleasant or
painful, is one of the surest ways to maintain
His presence with you. Nothing is so bad that
it could not have been worse; find the good in
everything instead of dwelling on the bad.
The negative usually precedes the positive,
and the two together are powerful when you
move from one to the other in His presence.

After following this habit of always referring everything to my Lord for years and
years, it has become almost second nature
with me. Yet I find the human element too
often present, for which I need to ask forgiveness, and I also ask the love and patience of my
fellow Christians.

Daily getting into the Word of God and daily
being in His presence brings me to great
humility and patience with myself and with
others.

My affirmation: "I keep the Lord always
before me; because he is at my right hand, I
shall not be moved" (Psalm 16:8).

Review

Group Sharing

1. How was the drudgery of Brother
   Lawrence's work transformed?
2. What is "The Game of Minutes"?

3. Name three results of praise which Frank Laubach found.
4. Share your own experience of Christ within, or of pray-walking, or of pray-working.
5. What things do you have in your home to remind you of Jesus?

Group Activity

Ask someone to read the following meditation while the others experience it with closed eyes. Pause between each step as you read John 15:1-12.

1. Picture in your mind a tree familiar to you.
2. Imagine that you are one of the branches, and that the smaller branches on your limb are your family and friends.
3. Imagine that the trunk is Jesus, and that His life-giving sap is flowing freely into you.
4. Now imagine the results. Choose your season of the year. Closing prayer: Stand up, hold hands, and give thanks, audibly, in short sentences for what was important to you in the meditation time.

Meditation for Chapter 5

I bind unto myself today
   The strong Name of the Trinity,
By invocation of the same,
   The Three in One, and One in Three.

Christ be with me, Christ within me,
   Christ behind me, Christ before me,
Christ beside me, Christ to win me,
   Christ to comfort and restore me,
Christ beneath me, Christ above me,
   Christ in quiet, Christ in danger,
Christ in hearts of all that love me,
   Christ in mouth of friend and stranger.

I bind myself the Name,
   The strong Name of the Trinity;
By invocation of the same,
   The Three in One, and One in Three,
Of whom all nature hath creation;
   Eternal Father, Spirit, Word:
Praise to the Lord of my salvation;
   Salvation is of Christ the Lord.

                —Saint Patrick

CHAPTER 5

Why the Deity of Our Lord Is Important

For to us a child is born,
   to us a son is given;
and the government will be upon
   his shoulder,
and his name will be called
"Wonderful Counsellor, Mighty God,
Everlasting Father, Prince of Peace"
(Isaiah 9:6).

"I and the Father are one." The Jews took up stones again to stone him. Jesus answered them, "I have shown you many good works from the Father; for which of these do you stone me?" The Jews answered him, "We stone you for no good work but for blasphemy; because you, being a man, make yourself God" (John 10:30-33).

"Have I been with you so long, and yet you do not know me, Philip? He who has seen me has seen the Father; how can you say, "Show us the Father?" (John 14:9).

Why is this chapter important?
Why is knowing that Jesus Christ is "very God of very God," as the Nicene Creed states, an

important truth in our faith and in our prayer life?

I can start with two reasons: The first is that when I teach to "pray to Jesus from the child in your heart" I'm always being asked, "Is Jesus Christ God? Didn't Jesus teach us to pray to our Father?"

The second reason is that I've been using the names "Jesus" and "God" interchangeably in these first four chapters. If these questions bother you, then in this chapter I'll share with you what I believe the Bible teaches.

Who Is Jesus Christ?

If Jesus Christ is not God, then how can we pray to Him? If He is only a man and not God, how can He love everybody in this world? If He is not God, how can He forgive sins? How could He take the sins of the whole world upon Himself?

If He is not the promised Messiah, who is He? In His lifetime they called him crazy, out of his mind; they said He was possessed by a demon. And today, many do not believe He is God. They call Him merely a prophet and a good man.

No one in his right mind would make the claims Jesus made. He said "I am the way"—not "I will teach you what the way is." He said, "I am the life and the resurrection . . . I am the vine . . . I am the door to the sheepfold . . . I am the bread of life . . . I am the true vine."

The question "Is Jesus God?" is one that unbelievers or the untaught usually ask. If a person wants to become a believer, he believes on the Lord Jesus Christ as a *Person* and not merely as a doctrine.

The answers are not easily accepted, for it means turning around from one's own way and becoming a follower or believer in Jesus. It means discipleship and obedience as one goes on, and that means, among other things, getting into the whole Bible and finding out more about Jesus.

What the Bible Says

The Bible teaches us that Jesus Christ is the Messiah, the Son of God, one with His Father, the Lamb of God who takes away the sin of the world. This truth was prophesied in the Old Testament (Isaiah 9:6), and that prophecy is now sung by choirs at Christmastime in the form of the *Messiah*, which ends with the glorious Hallelujah Chorus.

The whole Bible is the story of God, our Creator, who became a human being to show us what He is really like and to tell us how He became the lamb of God, our sin-bearer.

A careful reading of any New Testament in modern language will soon show you the multitude of subjects that Jesus taught His disciples, all of them based on the new commandment of love and forgiveness rather than on the Old Testament law, which demanded death and punishment for breaking any part of the law.

The Jews expected their Messiah to come as a conquering King rather than as a suffering servant of mankind or as an itinerant preacher who chose a few unlearned disciples.

Those who believed in Him were those who "had ears to hear," as He said in many of His parables. Today, those whose hearts are drawn by the Holy Spirit will respond. When you respond to the love of God as shown through Jesus Christ our Lord, you will believe.

Like doubting Thomas of old, who said that unless he saw the scars of the nails in Jesus' hands, and put his finger right on those scars, he would not believe that Jesus had risen from the dead.

Eight days later Jesus appeared to His disciples while they were in a room with all the doors closed. He said, "Peace be with you."

Then He said to Thomas, "Put your finger here, and see my hands, and put your hand and place it in my side; do not be faithless, but believing."

Thomas answered him, "My Lord and my God!"

Jesus said to him, "Have you believed because you have seen me? Blessed are those who have not seen and yet believe." (See John 20:24-29.) The next verse says this:

> Now Jesus did many other signs in the presence of his disciples, which are not written in this book; but these are written that you may believe that Jesus is the Christ, the Son of God, and that believing you may have life in his name (John 20:30).

Who Is This Man?

In the above verses, the Christ and the Son of God are both used as names of Jesus. *Christ* means "the Messiah" and Jesus used "son of man" often in referring to Himself; it is a term from prophetic passages in the Old Testament.

In Jewish culture, the son has the same rights, privileges, and honors that the father has. They were considered equals. This is not true in today's culture, and we must remember the Jewish interpretation of that day.

By calling God His Father, Jesus implied to the people that He was making Himself equal with God. That is why they assumed that He had blasphemed their law and ought to die. And die He did—for teaching the truth of who He is. But He Himself said that He came to give His life, to lay down His life, and He taught that He would rise again victorious over sin, death, and Satan. And He did.

To Whom Shall We Pray?

Didn't Jesus teach us to pray to the Father? Yes, He did, and today we call this the Lord's Prayer. He taught us to pray to our Father in secret, who would reward us openly as a rebuke to those who made a big show of praying on prayer-rugs in the street or wherever they were when the temple prayer-bell rang.

We can pray to any member of our triune God, who is one God. In the Book of Common Prayer, almost every *collect* starts, Almighty God . . . and ends with . . . through Jesus Christ our Lord, who liveth and reigneth with thee and the Holy Spirit, one God, forever and ever. Amen. The Trinity is a mystery. Illustrations which satisfy an ordinary person can be pulled apart by an expert philosopher.[1] Like H_2O, the formula for water has three forms: water, ice, steam and each a separate function. Or, relationships: a man is at the same time a

[1] For more explanation, read *The Trinity*, by Robert Crossley, InterVarsity Press, Downers Grove, Illinois 60615.

son, a brother, a father, a husband and never gets the roles confused.

The Claims Jesus Made

We have briefly covered the case for the question "Is Jesus Christ God?" from what the Bible teaches and from what His disciples believed.

Now let us consider the other question: "Didn't Jesus teach us to pray to our Father?" Does that mean we cannot pray to any other member of the Godhead?

We have already stated many of the claims that Jesus made regarding who He is. However, think for a moment what might have happened if He had come out openly and declared, "I am one with Jehovah-God. I am Jehovah. After I have suffered, died, and risen again, I will be praying for you, and you may freely pray to me."

He came very close to saying this, and actually it was what He meant.

The Jewish scholars couldn't believe their ears. They asked, "Who do you claim to be? Who do you think you are?"

His reply angered them, and they took up stones again, for they knew what He was saying and what it meant: He was calling God His Father. He repeatedly taught "I and the Father are one." Now notice that He goes even farther, and uses the holy, revered name of Jehovah-God of their sacred Scriptures (the Old Testament), which name no Jewish priest or scholar even dared say aloud.

That name is "I AM" (Exodus 3:14).

Jesus said, "Truly, truly, I say to you, before Abraham was, I AM." (See John 8:48-59.)

The Living Bible puts this in plain English, which was what it meant to the Jews of that day: "The absolute truth is that I was in existence before Abraham was ever born!" (See John 8:58 TLB.) When they tried to stone Him, he disappeared from the temple, for His time had not yet come. But they knew, and He knew.

In the tenth chapter of John the same issue arose when Jesus gave the discourse on "I am the good shepherd who lays down his life for the sheep . . . I and my Father are one." (See John 10:11,14,15,30-33.)

When Jesus asked them for which good work done in His Father's name they were going to stone Him, they replied, "We stone you for no good work but for blasphemy; because you, being a man, make yourself God" (John 10:33).

The deity of our Lord is a great mystery: that God became man to live and die among us, to be our sin-bearer, to love and redeem us and make us His own children.

It took the great Apostle Paul, converted to Christ and versed in all the Jewish Scriptures, to bring the Old and New Covenants together in his letters to the churches. This is what we know as the "gospel," the good news.

In celebrating the mass or the Eucharist, people repeat together with conviction:

Christ has died.
Christ has risen.
Christ will come again.

In conclusion, having stated the case as simply as possible, we ought to pray to Jesus, who is God the Son, as well as to God the Father, and God the Holy Spirit. I hope you follow through on the review questions and activities, and make these truths your own.

We are writing this that
your joy may be complete
(1 John 1:4).

Review

Group Sharing

1. What two questions are often stumbling blocks to praying?
2. Go through this chapter and list the names used to identify Jesus. Use them later for personal worship.
3. What claims did Jesus make for Himself? How were they received?

Group Activity

1. Ask the group to divide into partners.
2. Take turns asking one another these questions, and use the answers given in this chapter:

   a) Why do you believe that Jesus is God?

   b) Didn't Jesus teach us to pray *"Our Father"*?

3. Pray together, asking in faith, for an opportunity to meet and talk to someone who needs these truths before your next meeting.

Meditation for Chapter 6

Gracious Spirit, dwell with me!
　I myself would gracious be;
And with words that help and heal
　Would Thy life in mine reveal;
And with actions bold and meek
　Would for Christ, my Savior, speak.
Truthful Spirit, dwell with me!
　I myself would truthful be;
And with wisdom kind and clear
　Let Thy life in mine appear;
And with actions brotherly
　Speak my Lord's sincerity.

　　　　　　　　　　—Thomas T. Lynch

CHAPTER 6

Obedience to the Holy Spirit

How does one know the difference between the voice of the Spirit within and the voice of one's own desires? How does one go about finding his vocation, or rather, God's plan for his or her life? Or finding a life partner? Or facing the loss of a loved one? Or discovering one's gifts, or knowing which home to buy, which business to invest in, which trips to take, which college to attend . . . ?

For years I distrusted my own desires because I wrongly interpreted Psalm 37:4: *Delight thyself in the Lord, and He shall give thee the desires of thine heart* (KJV). I thought this meant that God would take away what I wanted and put His desires there instead. Maybe it did mean that, but I never could tell the difference, so I never trusted my own feelings. I'll be sharing with you how God taught me that when I was surrendered to His will and delighted in His ways, He gave me desires which were one with His desires for me.

My First Lesson in Guidance

My first lesson in guidance came from my mother, who was a woman of faith and prayer. When I was perplexed about how I could make a total surrender regarding things in the future, she gave me this illustration.

Imagine two baskets in front of you. One is covered and one is uncovered. The open one contains all the things I know about now, all the things I would like to have or be. Those I should yield, one by one (and name them), in prayer to Jesus; then He could live within me and guide me to His perfect way. The covered basket contains all the things which would come up over the years which I didn't know about now. I was to say one big YES to all that was in both baskets, but would need to say many small YESes through the years as decisions presented themselves.

At the age of 15 I had such a powerful conversion that I now believe I was filled with the Spirit at the same time. Many gifts of the Spirit became evident very soon. The surrender my mother was outlining for me was a joy to make, especially when I read Romans 12:1,2.

> I appeal to you therefore, brethren, by the mercies of God, to present your bodies as a living sacrifice, holy, and acceptable to God, which is your spiritual worship. Do not be conformed to this world but be transformed by the renewal of your mind, that you may prove what is the will of God, what is good and acceptable and perfect.

If you have a Living Bible, read those verses in the paraphrase given there, as they carry an even more beautiful promise of total fulfillment.

Three Well-Known Tests for Guidance

1. God speaks to us personally through His Word.
2. He speaks through His Spirit in our hearts.
3. He sends helping (or hindering) circumstances.

Jesus said, "If you obey my teaching you are really my disciples; you will know the truth, and the truth will make you free" (John 8:31,32 TEV). He also said, "If you abide in me, and my words abide in you, ask whatever you will, and it shall be done for you" (John 15:7).

To abide or live in the will of God is the only way to bring joy to one's heart, peace to one's mind, and fulfillment to one's life. To live with God, to listen to His voice, to accept His will is a lovely way to live— and peaceful, too. The aftereffects of obedience far outweigh the aftereffects of disobedience.

There are people who open the Bible at random, put their finger on a verse, and take that as guidance. It has been known to work, but unless all three tests are evident and bring peace, I don't recommend it. Even the devil knew how to quote Scripture to Jesus when He was tempted!

My First Experiences in Guidance

I probably had some small experiences in guidance, but the first big one came upon my graduation from high school. I wanted to find the will of God for my next step, and naturally

I thought of college. The very same camp meeting where I was converted found me kneeling with a group of young people dedicating my life to God's service. That was after a missionary from China spoke to us, so it wasn't too strange that after four years my life-call was to China.

My parents were both college graduates, so why not I too? However, they were influenced by our pastor and his wife, who felt strongly that Rosalind should attend a Bible school first so that her faith would be strongly grounded, and not turned aside by nonbelieving professors. What choice did I really have? It seemed right, and I hadn't yet learned the three steps of being guided by the Holy Spirit.

How wonderfully our loving Father over-rules and makes Romans 8:28 come to pass so that "all things do work together for good to those who love the Lord." It was during those two years that I faced both the question of my life-partner and my lifework.

A certain young man professed to be in love with me and wanted to marry me. I wasn't exactly in love, but I was powerfully curious about it all, and so I prayed about it.

At about the same time, in one of our classes, we were required to read a book that changed everything for me. The life of J. Hudson Taylor, founder of the China Inland Mission, made such a powerful impact upon me that I left the class and went to my own room. An intelligent Chinese youth had asked Mr. Taylor how long he had known the truth about God, and when he learned that it was family knowledge handed down for generations, he said, "Why did it take you so long to get over here?"

Suddenly there was no such word as *heathen* anymore, but only searching Chinese youth who needed to hear about Jesus. I remember praying on my knees, "Lord, I haven't any gifts at all to offer You, but at least I can talk; I can tell others about You." I can't begin to describe my sense of calling (yet of unworthiness) and the breaking of my heart over all who had never heard about Jesus Christ. I only knew that the cost of going to China was spread before me: leaving my home, my parents, my brothers and sisters, my homeland, my boyfriend—yes, and college too . . . and maybe even a home of my own.

I opened my Bible for a verse, and there it was—Exodus 19:5,6: "Now therefore, if ye will obey my voice indeed, and keep my covenant, then ye shall be a peculiar treasure unto me above all people: for all the earth is mine. And ye shall be unto me a kingdom of priests and a holy nation" (KJV).

And another verse—Mark 8:34,35: "If any man would come after me, let him deny himself and take up his cross and follow me. For whoever would save his life will lose it, and whoever loses his life for my sake and the gospel's will save it."

I was 19 years old at the time I made this consecration and accepted this call, leaving all the details up to the Lord, which He within that very year worked out for me. I even saw myself sailing to China (as in a vision) on a big white ocean liner, and I'd never seen one of these in my life. Great peace came to me, and as I shared this experience with friends, great joy and affirmation came also.

Except . . . that young man was out of the picture; he had no intention of going to China. While I'm on that subject, the Lord and I have had quite a controversy over that subject through the years, always ending in my submission and willingness to delight in His will and to walk in His ways . . . plus asking forgiveness for my own ways.

Very soon I began to see the three tests fulfilled so that I could follow His guidance: 1) the Word, which I've already told you about; 2) the witness of the Spirit, which was bringing unspeakable peace to me; 3) then circumstances opened, when Rev. and Mrs. E. R. Munroe of Canton, South China (The Oriental Missionary Society), invited me to go back with them as a missionary secretary. There I was at the age of 20, on the Empress of Canada sailing for China, and it was white! I knew I was in the will of the Lord.

Later Lessons in Obedience

During my two terms in China, I was taught many lessons about obedience and guidance, and the need for testing the choices as they came.

1. I learned to be content and satisfied there in that office and to give it my best until another door opened.

2. I learned to step out in obedience when I

couldn't see the way. After nine years in that office and through surgery and prolonged rest, I heard the inner voice telling me it was time now to go into China's villages and tell them about Jesus—there was my original call!

3. I was stripped of security, because in our mission the missionaries either taught in the Bible institute or worked in the office. The trained Chinese youth went into the harvest fields. If I accepted this call as from the Lord, it would mean that I would leave the OMS and go where? In a foreign country, with no support and no co-workers? Lord, what are You saying to me? I was learning to trust God alone.

4. I learned the value of a prayer partner. Esther Erny prayed for me and with me, encouraging me to obey that inner Voice.

5. Prayer was answered, and guidance was confirmed. The OMS created a new ministry: they sent me out with four trained young women into the rural villages of North China to assist the local pastors.

Our Unseen Enemy

We were in enemy territory, and we had the promise, "Not by might, nor by power, but by my Spirit, saith the Lord." So began my new career of teaching others about our great God, and His Son, our Saviour Jesus Christ. Maybe someday I'll write in more detail about the leading of God's Spirit during those days.

We were encouraged by the careful reading of Paul's letters to the early churches. We discovered that they were written to Spirit-filled believers, teaching them to live in obedience to that Spirit, to make Christ known; and rebuking them for actions outside the guidance of His Spirit.

In the chapter on Prayer Partners, I'll go further into this teaching, showing how Jesus taught us to pray regarding evil around us.

What If We Make a Mistake?

First of all, I've learned that Jesus Christ redeems our mistakes and teaches us valuable lessons through them. However, the pride of man is an effective tool when it comes to hindering, thwarting, and preventing the work of the Holy Spirit and the will of God (which are synonymous), both in our personal lives and in the whole Body of Christ.

The Acts of the Apostles is full of illustrations of how the Holy Spirit led members of the early church, and how they obeyed or disobeyed Him. As a young believer I remember reading Acts 5:32, which alarmed me: "We are witnesses to these things, and so is the Holy Spirit, whom God has given to those who obey him."

I also remember thinking, "How in God's wide world was I to be sure I was always obeying the Holy Spirit? "Quench not the Spirit," Paul wrote to the Thessalonians. Not obeying Him would be quenching the Spirit. How could I know the difference between "people" ways and God's ways when so many religious people were ready to tell me what to do? How would I know when the Holy Spirit was speaking to me?

I finally came to the place where I told the Lord that I would rather obey Him and make mistakes than disobey Him and do nothing. And that did happen. But always in my heart I knew that He knew; moreover, I saw how He redeemed and used every failure I ever had in ways beyond my expectations.

Three Things Which Hinder the Spirit

A few years ago I saw a large poster which immediately got my attention and caused me to see more clearly the hand of God, not only in my own life, but in the lives of those who came to me for counseling. I was walking through the parish hall of my church (St. James Episcopal, Newport Beach, CA) when I stopped short. I not only read the poster several times, but I got out my purse notebook and copied it.

1. Man's pride (in being right, going one's own way)
2. Failure to use the gifts given to one. -
3. Failure to catch the whole vision.

I'm still working on those three, but they have enlightened many things in my past life. I'm more grateful every day that when Jesus left this world, He promised not to leave us alone but to send His Holy Spirit to be our Comforter, our Counselor, our Guide, and our Helper.

This is part of getting the most out of your prayer life—letting the Spirit teach you about past events, letting Him pull things together to show you the love and care that your heavenly Father has always had for you.

I love chapters 14 to 17 in John's Gospel, and I read and reread them.

Further Guidance:
Second and Third Careers

Early in this chapter I mentioned that I would tell you about how God taught me that my desires for His will were not always the best. They might be good, but not His best.

At the end of 14 years as a missionary to China (although I will always be Chinese at heart), while on furlough, I was notified that the China personnel were to be drastically cut. That meant looking for another place to serve my Lord. There were three choices before me:

1. Work among the Chinese in Chicago.
2. Speak in churches which were calling me.
3. Finish my college work.

Naturally I chose the first, but it petered out—there was no opening at all. The second one lasted three years, but it was the third one which God used to lead me into my next career. My life-call to minister the truth regarding Jesus Christ has never changed, and in all the major changes in my life, I can trace the guiding, loving hand of my Lord.

The opening to finish college came through circumstances so plain that I couldn't rationalize them away. Two-and-a-half years later I received my B.A. degree from Asbury College in Witmore, Kentucky.

Once more the guidance of the Spirit came through circumstances as friends in Canada, Rhea and Kathleen Snider, guided me and prayed for me. I was accepted as a staff member of Inter-Varsity Christian Fellowship in the Pacific Northwest states and so began a most fulfilling and fruitful 14 years.

The disciplines I had in both the OMS and IVCF were guidelines for me as my third career opened up after that, as a free-lance writer and speaker. I learned simplicity and poverty from the Chinese, and now through student work the gift of teaching became evident.

Then the door opened (in churches of every denomination) for me to write and teach what I had learned. The open door this time came when Eugenia Price sent me to Zondervan Publishing House in Grand Rapids. There the editorial staff gave me a contract to sign even though they had never seen a single line I had written!

I was 50 years old, and I marveled at the faithfulness of God and the guidance of the Spirit which had been given to me all those years. I am presently writing my fourteenth book, and I speak in 60 to 80 churches and conferences yearly.

Choosing the Best Instead of the Good

Thanks and praise be to the Lord for His guiding Spirit, and for a heart to delight in His ways, which are always the best ways! I must say that this was not without conflict, indecision, loneliness, and failure, as I sorted out the will of God and obeyed that inner Voice.

I am reminded of a story about "good ways" which our pastor told one Sunday. In a certain vestry meeting the members had carefully and lengthily discussed a certain problem. Finally one of them summarized, "I believe that we have come to a reasonable conclusion which we ought to accept and vote on." A quiet voice spoke up, "Yes, but I do not believe we have found God's way." That took courage.

My Tests for Finding God's Best Way

The good and the better can become the enemy of the best, because of man's pride. My way may seem good, and your way may seem better, but how about God's way? Our unseen enemy uses our pride to hinder us from seeking and finding the will of God.

1. Has the Lord given me direction through His Word? Through His Spirit? Through circumstances? Through humbleness on my part to obey?
2. Is this proposed action compatible with the character and Person of Jesus Christ? Am I making this decision out of my own pride or because I desire to follow His guidance and with all my heart seek to be His obedient disciple?
3. In other words, is this the kindest, most

loving thing I can do at this time?
4. The result: If I am in God's best will, and
    trusting Him (even without seeing, even
    without security), there will be peace in
    my spirit (Colossians 3:15).

To Sum It All Up

I must be humble enough to put away my
pride and do what my Lord asks of me. Others
will not always agree with me, but deep in my
heart I must know that I am in His will. My
decision must be loving and kind, and, as far
as I can tell, it must glorify Jesus Christ. I can't
always give a good reason immediately, but I
must use the gifts He has given me to build up
the Body of Christ, and that means wherever
He sends me.

I made a covenant with the Lord when I first
started to hold prayer workshops, that I
would trust Him not to bring invitations I
could not accept; that I would accept every one
if I was able to work out the dates.

An important lesson I've learned during the
past few years is this: *God knew the answer
long before I knew there was a problem.* He is
both sovereign and loving (though often His
ways are inscrutable), but I know that He is ut-
terly trustworthy. The servant is not above his
Master. God's plan takes in the whole Body of
Christ, no matter what name they are called,
but especially those who know they are sinners and need a Saviour.

That includes me . . . and you.

Hearing the voice of the Lord is what our prayer life is all about.

How the Holy Spirit Helps Us

Question: Can we pray to the Holy Spirit?
Answer: Yes, because Jesus told us that He is our Helper (Romans 8:26).
Question: For what things may we pray to the Holy Spirit?
Answer: For the following things, which He does for us.

1. He assures us that we are children of God.
2. He intercedes for us because He knows the will of God.
3. He lives right within us to free us from the laws of sin and death.
4. He gives us power to witness and to serve Christ.
5. He teaches and instructs us about Christ.
6. He reminds us of what we already know and ought to do.
7. He guides us in finding our lifework or our life-partner, as well as all that pertains to our everyday living.
8. He gives us quiet trust and ability to wait.
9. He pours the love of God into our hearts.
10. He rebukes us when we miss God's plan or when we sin.
11. He gives us peace when we do God's will.

Scripture references for the above can be matched up (in your own study) from these passages: John 15:26; 14:26; 16:7-15; Acts 1:8; Romans 5:5. At least six of the above things are in Romans chapter 8. See also 1 Thessalonians 5:19; Colossians 3:15; Ephesians 4:20.

Review

Group Sharing

1. Divide into groups of three or four.
2. What are the three tests for guidance?
3. What three things hinder the Spirit?
4. Share an experience of guidance, either success or failure, with each other.

Group Activity

1. Now stand up, in a huddle, with arms around each other, and repeat Matthew 18:19,20.
2. Pray as honestly as you can (first person singular, "I") about something the Spirit may be telling you recently.
3. Pray for each other by name, and give thanks.

Meditation for Chapter 7

What a Friend we have in Jesus,
All our sins and griefs to bear!
What a privilege to carry
Everything to God in prayer!
O what peace we often forfeit,
O what needless pain we bear,
All because we do not carry
Everything to God in prayer!

Have we trials and temptations?
Is there trouble anywhere?
We should never be discouraged:
Take it to the Lord in prayer.
Can we find a friend so faithful,
Who will all our sorrows share?
Jesus knows our every weakness:
Take it to the Lord in prayer.

Are we weak and heavy-laden,
Cumbered with a load of care?
Jesus only is our refuge:
Take it to the Lord in prayer.
Do thy friends despise, forsake thee?
Take it to the Lord in prayer:
In His arms He'll take and shield thee!
Thou wilt find a refuge there.

—Joseph M. Scrivers

CHAPTER 7

The Sin Which Blocks Prayer

How important it is for us to have clean hearts when we approach the throne of God in prayer. This means that we must open ourselves to the searchlight of the Spirit, and be willing to admit where we have transgressed God's royal law of love.

Unrecognized guilt in the area of not loving our brother or of unforgiveness can be a huge mountain blocking out what that inner voice wants to say to us, either regarding ourselves or those for whom we pray. For who knows the mind of the Spirit, except the Spirit, who longs to pray through us for the will of God to be done on earth?

God's Great Mercy

How great is the loving-kindness and mercy of our great God! For which one of us is perfect in conduct before Him or before our brothers or sisters? Our intentions are known by Him, and somewhere there is a meeting place in the heart of God for justice and mercy.

He does not hold our transgressions against us, as His children, if we deal with them when our hearts condemn us. If we rationalize our sins away, His mercy is still extended to us until the day of reckoning comes; then in His time and in His way He will in faithfulness face us with our need to love our brothers and sisters.

In my study of the teachings of Jesus on prayer there are three things which stand out: 1) ask; 2) believe that you receive; 3) forgive your brother (Mark 11:22-25). In this passage in Mark's Gospel, Jesus teaches us not to back down or be afraid of that mountain in front of us.

What are your mountains? Or have you cast them all into the sea already? If you don't know them, you can't deal with them. The only way to know that all is well and clear between my Lord and me is to spend time in His presence.

The other day someone remarked to me, "There is nobody I know whom I don't forgive." I replied, "You mean that nobody has misjudged you, hurt you, maligned you, or slighted you?" "Oh, that's different," was the reply; "I think they need to forgive me."

No one suffered greater injustice than Jesus our Lord, and all that He took on Himself was for you and for me. Now He asks us to forgive, even as our heavenly Father forgives us.

"But," I hear someone say, "what if my heart does not condemn me? What if I've done all I can do, and already asked forgiveness, but the barrier still seems to be there?"

I'll say to you what my friend Anna B. Mow once said to me: "Rosalind, you tend to take 80 percent of the blame when only 20 percent is yours." That gave me a great deal of insight into myself, and yet I still have this tendency, at least until I've done all I know how to do. Then

I can leave it with my kind heavenly Father, who brings all things to light eventually. I can also pray for that particular person with a love which is cleansed and a heart which is forgiven, and I can wait.

Love and Forgiveness

The chapters in the New Testament which teach love to our brothers and sisters have always been my favorites, such as John 15, John 17, 1 Corinthians 13, and the whole First Letter of John.

But if our hearts condemn us, then what? Confession brings peace again: "If we confess our sins He is faithful and just to forgive us our sins, and to cleanse us from all unrighteousness" (1 John 1:9 KJV).

If our hearts do not condemn us? "My dear friends, if our heart does not condemn us, we have courage in God's presence. We receive from him whatever we ask, because we obey his commands and do what pleases him. This is what he commands that we believe in the name of his Son Jesus Christ and love one another, just as Christ commanded us" (1 John 3:21-23 TEV).

Here again, we see that asking in prayer is vitally connected with loving one another. Because God-given love is the cementing union of the Body of Christ, our enemy will use subtle ways which we fail to recognize to alienate us from one another. He does this in such a clever way that we stand on our own rights, and fail to recognize what is going on.

"She's on the Altar Guild, but she fails to show up, so I have to pinch-hit for her." (So you are calling her unreliable and patting yourself on the back?)

"He always uses that tone of voice when he talks to me, as if I needed correction." (It couldn't be your pride, could it?)

"I never seem to get included in their goings-on or their invitations." (Self-pity eats like a cancer.)

"Why in the world does he/she wear clothes like that to a worship service?" (Have you spoken to the offending one with love and after praying?)

"I wish he'd get his hair cut, or even wash it in the shower. It really offends me." (You name that one.)

"I think R____ plays the organ better than J_____, and I wish they'd ask R_____ more often." (Why are you taking sides?)

"If others in church only knew what I know about him." (Since when are you the judge?)

The Power of Confession

Martha, a friend of mine, told me this story about herself. For some years she was a church secretary, and one day as she was typing a list of names her heart suddenly jumped with almost physical pain as the Holy Spirit convicted her. That name — that man — she didn't love him and hadn't even tried to love him.

On numerous occasions she had watched him use his talents as a businessman to (in her estimation) manipulate the church board, "all for the good of the church," as he put it.

"I never prayed for him or even thought of praying. I never thought about the fact that I was holding all these things against him in my heart."

Unable to sit any longer at her desk, she went into the pastor's study. One look at her face told him something was wrong. They prayed together, and Martha received God's forgiveness for her failure to love and to forgive her brother.

A prayer burst from her lips: "God, be merciful to me, and to him." Peace came like a river.

That night with a small group she was able to pray the prayer of faith for her daughter-in-law, who was only 21 but was suffering from an unknown liver ailment. Jan began to improve and soon was completely healed. An unforgiving heart will hinder our prayers until it is dealt with.

When people say to me that the church is full of hypocrites, and so why should they attend, I respond by saying, "Who said the church was a museum for saints? It's a hospital for sinners." We are all sinners being saved—present tense—and we all need to admit our faults and receive forgiveness, that we may forgive one another and thus fulfill the commandment of Jesus: "Love one another as I have loved you."

Healing of Memories

This is becoming a familiar term to many of us today, as we see books being written on this subject and find lives being transformed who have experienced this inner healing.

Having experienced this healing myself, and having guided others in this same healing, I finally came to one conclusion: Healing of memories is nothing but old-fashioned confession. In a way it is a kind of psychotherapy which brings Jesus Christ into the picture with healing and love, instead of more guilt and confusion.

One does not have to dig around for "failures to love and forgive," because the Holy Spirit is a faithful Servant who brings light to our pathway and speaks to us about what needs to be taken care of. Being in the presence of Jesus Christ, loving Him, adoring Him, worshiping Him, and waiting there (sometimes without words) will open your heart to whatever He wants to say to you, whether it is confession of some specific sin (such as failure to love and forgive), failure to make peace with your brother, guidance to pray for someone, or instruction to move out in obedience to God's will.

> Little lamb, who lost thee?
>   I myself, none other.
> Little lamb, who found thee?
>   Jesus, Shepherd, Brother.
> Ah, Lord, what I cost thee?
>   Canst thou still desire?
> Still my arms surround thee,
>   Still I lift thee higher,
> Draw thee nigher.
>
> —Christine Rosetti

The teaching of our Lord on the subject of forgiveness is the only place where I've found that any sin of mine could keep my prayers from being heard.[1] Being human, and often blind to one's own failures, it takes the powerful moving of the Holy Spirit to reveal the sinfulness of our own hearts, especially when it comes to failure to love and to forgive.

The Bible has one cure: Face up, confess, repent, and make peace with your brother.

The Dynamics of Confession

Did you ever watch a guilty child, and then observe the difference after he admitted what he had done? Such release, such freedom, such joy on his face and in his voice!

As adults we should be aware that there is such a thing as false guilt, which needs to be distinguished from true guilt.

False guilt can settle on us like a dark cloud and steal all our freedom away. We seem to be full of condemnation and depression for no apparent reason.

True guilt comes from the Lord, who longs that we walk in obedience with clean hearts before Him. You can always tell the difference, because when you go and ask Him about those feelings, He will point out exactly what is wrong. There will be something specific for you to deal with; and when you do, the peace will return to your heart.

---

[1]Mark 11:25,26.

Sometimes we make each other feel guilty for reasons that we are not even willing to face. This happens in families, in business, and even in our churches. We blame others and lay a guilt trip on them for what is or is not going on in our lives. We blame people who have done nothing, in order to ease our own guilt. We blame the bad weather, our unsuitable job, our overweight, our lack of opportunity, our lack of education, or our lack of ready cash.

The cause of such rationalization is not too hard to locate—your own poor self-image. When you don't love yourself, you can't love another person, nor can you love the Lord your God with your whole heart.

Do you need to forgive God for being born? Do you need to forgive your mother or your father for something? Or your sister or your brother? Or your son or your daughter? Or your wife or your husband?

As children of God, having been forgiven our sins, we should be quick to hear the Spirit when He points out failures which need to be admitted, confessed, and even made right with the other party. We should be quick to repent, quick to forgive, and quick to give or receive forgiveness from another person.

In my book *Within the Circle of God's Love*, I have two chapters on the subject of confession. In some detail I share my own experience of how the Lord broke down my resistance to confession.

It happened while I was in China. There were two persons who turned away without speaking whenever I was around. I had no condemnation (which proved nothing) until I studied this subject and read carefully what Jesus taught on this subject of forgiving others: He really took care of all eventualities! Such as: whether I had offended knowingly or unknowingly, or whether another person had done the same to me.

Read these passages in your own Bible.

When my brother/sister has something against me:	) Matthew) 5:23,24,43-48
When I have something against my brother/sister	) Matthew) 18:15-17,21-35

When is one responsible to act on making peace or asking forgiveness? Just as soon as one is aware of it, and when, after praying, guidance is given on how to do it, where, and even when. Yes, I made peace with those two persons, and I learned more about my own stupid faults which offend others and which I've asked God to help me correct.

What if the other person cannot see your viewpoint and does not accept your apology? That is the time for you to exercise the royal law of love, and to pray for him or her each time that person's name comes to mind. Pray for him as you would want someone to pray for you, as in Ephesians 3:14-21.

God's Direction for Us

Matthew 18, the whole chapter, contains Jesus' teaching on being childlike and forgiving one another. And with this teaching are three of the most important verses he gave us on the subject of prayer.

They are verses 18-20: "Truly I say to you, whatever you bind on earth shall be bound in heaven, and whatever you loose on earth will be loosed in heaven. Again I say to you, if two of you agree on earth about anything they ask, it will be done for them by my Father in heaven. For where two or three are gathered in my name, there am I in the midst of them."

These are the verses on which much of my teaching on conversational prayer is based. (More on this in chapter 9.)

With that precious promise of the presence of Christ with us as we pray, what reason can we continue to hold for not loving our brother? Our Lord does not ask us for anything except to love one another as He has loved us, and so to give the life-giving acceptance that is often the difference between health and sickness.

We are asked to show our love for God by our love for one another. This is the real proof of our love for Him. We can never be closer to God or more like Him than when we let Him give us all the love we need for ourselves and for one another. In fact, when we look at the Biblical teaching closely, we find that it is more important to be loving and forgiving than it is to be loved.

Because the fruit of the Holy Spirit is love, we can be filled with that love and can let it overflow wherever it is needed.

Let the love of God break through your

resistance and your unbelief; dare to step out and make peace by forgiving your God, yourself, and your fellowman.

> Let everyone speak the truth with his neighbor, for we are members of one another ... and be kind to one another, tenderhearted, forgiving one another, as God in Christ forgave you (Ephesians 4:25,32).

Review

Group Activity

1. Love is not love until you give it away. "Lord, where have I failed to give away love or to give forgiveness?" With pencil in hand, divide your paper into ten-year periods of your life.
2. Quietly, unhurriedly, during one period daily, ask the Holy Spirit to throw light upon the forgotten past, and to bring to your mind those persons from whom you are estranged, no matter whose fault it was, or where you still find hurt and bitterness.
3. The inner voice of the Spirit will show you where to start, how to pray, and what the next step should be. Some may have gone home to heaven. Which ones need a word or letter of apology? Or an invitation from you long withheld?
4. As you pray, visualize that person. See the

healing love of God surrounding him or her, as well as your love and forgiveness, thus giving the Spirit a fresh opportunity in that life (and in yours).

5. If you mean business, my advice is to share this list with your spiritual advisor or a trusted friend. If I had learned this earlier, I would have saved myself from some embarrassing admissions which I later learned were unnecessary. Trust the Lord to guide you, and wait until He does. If He does not give you immediate guidance, know even then that your prayers are opening doors both in your heart and in the heart of the other person.

6. The keys to answered prayer: love and forgiveness.

Meditation for Chapter 8

I heard the voice of Jesus say,
  "Come unto Me and rest;
Lay down, thou weary one,
  Lay down thy head upon My breast."
I came to Jesus as I was,
  Weary and worn and sad;
I found in Him a resting place,
  And He has made me glad.

I heard the voice of Jesus say,
  "Behold, I freely give
The living water; thirsty one,
  Stoop down, and drink and live."
I came to Jesus, and I drank
  Of that life-giving stream;
My thirst was quenched, my soul revived,
  And now I live in Him.

I heard the voice of Jesus say,
  "I am the dark world's Light;
Look unto me, thy morn shall rise,
  And all thy day be bright."
I looked to Jesus and I found
  In Him my star, my Sun;
And in that Light of Life I'll walk,
  Till travelling days are done.

                —Horatius Bonar

CHAPTER 8

How Our Spiritual Lives Are Affected by Stress

Those who are committed disciples of Christ believe Romans 8:28—that all things work together for good to those who love God. At the same time we are aware of the multiplied demands that daily living places upon us, until we are victims of stress before we know it. Since my judgment is faulty, I am often at fault and so need to spend time with my Lord daily and draw upon His life within me all day long in order to maintain my spiritual and physical health.

Everything we think, do, say, or eat affects some part of our body—that miraculous gift which God gave to mankind when He created us. Yet how seldom in our religious or church classes are we instructed about dealing with the stresses which life hands each of us.

The human body is a miracle of divine engineering, with a built-in heating/cooling system, a self-immunizing system, a hormone-producing system, and a reproductive system, to say nothing of the complicated nervous and digestive systems. All of these are regulated by the mastermind within us called the brain.

Added to these physical processes, the Lord our God has provided for our emotional needs by giving us various capacities for enjoyment, the greatest of which is love.

Love or Perish is the name of a book I read

years ago. To withhold love from children is to stunt their maturity. It is better to love than to wait for someone to love us. It is still better for us to receive the love of the Lord, so that we can then be in touch with the source of love and can share His love and ours with other people.

When either our physical or emotional needs become driving, consuming desires, they can get us into grievous trouble—trouble that makes us forget the Lord our God . . . or did we forget Him before that? Trouble that sends us to Him for answers to our prayers. Trouble that also sends us to seek medical aid.

In other words, it results in trouble which triggers emotional or physical problems because we have ignored our feelings and have centered on getting the cure. The causes within ourselves, within our own minds or bodies, are ignored until we are distressed beyond measure and are forced to take stock of what is really going on.

We will look into only a few of the more common ailments which incapacitate or plague us, pinpointing a few causes and feelings, and facing up to them. Then we can be in a better position to cooperate mentally, to make a few decisions with the help of the Lord God, and we can be on our way to health and wholeness.

Common Ailments Which Distress Us

Stress: A physical, chemical, or emotional factor that causes bodily or mental tension and may be a factor in causing disease; overreaction to ordinary events.

All of life brings stress, and good stress is needed if one is to adjust successfully to life's demands. The key to whether stress affects us in a healthy or unhealthy way lies in our own mental attitude toward circumstances, ourselves, and any other party involved, including the Lord our God.

Common symptoms of stress: Headaches, cramps in the stomach, poor elimination, tension, dizziness, insomnia, and anxiety, which in turn lead to fatigue, frustration, and depression. This all adds up to more physical and emotional distress.

Continued physical symptoms of distress: There are some people who live to a ripe old age without any of these symptoms, but such people are rare today. Our retirement and nursing homes are full of people waiting to die through hypertension (high blood pressure), obesity, ulcers, colitis, arthritis, and many other diseases.

Common emotions which distress: Any of these feelings, if allowed to harbor in us produce some kind of fear (which is opposite to love): resentment, anxiety, regret, the death-wish, jealousy, guilt, or hatred of self, parents, or others. Prolonged tension or any emotional crisis such as divorce, continual changing of jobs or residences, or loss of loved ones will bring feelings of despair which God alone has the power to heal, and which, if they become chronic, can result in physical or emotional diseases.

Options Open for Healing

The human body has within it the power to heal itself when our minds cooperate and our spirits are in tune with the Lord our Maker and our Healer. Thanks be to Him for all the medical, surgical, and spiritual help already available!

The title of this chapter could have been "How Our Emotions Affect Our Spiritual Lives and Hinder Our Prayers." Go into any bookstore or health store today and you'll find shelves full of books on nutrition, good health, and self-help. A surprising number of them recommend meditation and faith in God.

While most M.D.'s will admit that many of our physical problems are triggered by our emotions, they are reluctant to treat the causes, but usually deal only with the symptoms. People are willing to pay from 60 to 200 dollars per hour for a qualified psychiatrist to listen to their story, help them sort things out, and try to put meaning back into their lives.

There are only a few clinics today where the whole person is diagnosed, where Christ is part of the answer, and where emotional as well as physical causes are treated. Change comes slowly, and it could be many more years before such treatment is commonly available.

We need to look at both the positive and the negative sides of our personal problems, which will give us expectation and hope (two lifesavers) as we begin to face our problems honestly in prayer (preferably with a counselor who is in touch with God).

God will show you the next step to take. Priorities which have been ignored can then be located. A spirit-filled disciple is just as subject to human negatives as an unbeliever, perhaps even more vulnerable—but with all of God's resources available.

Norman Grubb points out: "It is a law of the universe that a positive must have its negative to manifest through. So don't dare say you are a 'block' to God, or 'need to get out of the way.' Stay in the way! As human negatives we always have to start by being hurt or bothered or resenting or resisting confusion or fear. That makes us live negatives instead of just dead wood! But then, we don't condemn ourselves or try to change or regard our negative stirrings as a hindrance. No, they are stepping stones. They motivate us to transfer our believings from being attached to what is hurting us to seeing Jesus by faith right at the center of that dark spot, just as He was at the center of the cross, and came out as our resurrected Lord! This helps us to accept ourselves as His necessary negatives. And if on occasions we stay too long stewing in our negatives, well, thank God for eternal forgiveness in Christ! And let's get up and get going again!" (from a personal letter).

God's Program for Health

A good counselor who loves God and trusts

in the power of God is to be sought after like a pearl of great price. A Christian psychologist or a Spirit-filled priest or pastor or a friend who has been through the process we know today as "healing of memories" can be of invaluable assistance. This is really confession and absolution reaching into our deepest memories.

A lawyer tested Jesus with this question: "Teacher, which is the great commandment in the law?" Jesus' answer is told in both the Old and New Testaments:

Thou shalt love the Lord thy God with all thy heart, and with all thy soul, and with all thy mind. This is the first and great commandment. And the second is like unto it: Thou shalt love thy neighbor as thyself. On these two commandents hang all the law and the prophets. (Matthew 22:37-40 KJV).

The Human Breakdown

Our lifestyle today is geared to ever-increasing speed, and some of us live a rat-race, with not enough hours in the day. I've said that about myself many times. The right word for that is *overachieving*. Another word could be *idolatry*, which is putting something in the rightful place which only the Lord our God is meant to occupy. Daily guidance from Him, daily communion with Him, and our willingness to obey Him is a simple formula, but with a price attached: "Take up your cross and follow me." Failure to follow or heed that inner voice leads us to many follies from which we suffer until our spirits are healed.

In the meantime we try medicine, surgery, and faith healings, but sometimes the disease progresses so far that only the ultimate healing—when God takes us home—brings relief.

In the following pages you will find true stories about distressing diseases and attempts to find the cause: paralysis, colitis, ulcers, arthritis, and skin rash.

Paralysis

I recall a trip I made in my early ministry to a Canadian city, where I spoke in a rural church. As the people gathered, I saw a stretcher being rolled in. After the meeting was over, I asked about the woman on that stretcher. I was told that she was totally paralyzed, and had been for several years. I spoke to her and prayed for her. At that time I knew little of the power of agreeing in prayer or a healing prayer, but my heart was filled with compassion, and I assured her of God's love.

Some years later, word came to me that this woman had been completely healed and was walking around perfectly normal.

Then I heard the story. It seems that her parents, upon their death, had left all the inheritance to the older sister, asking her to share with the younger as they would have done. The older sister withheld most of it, thus incurring the deep anger and animosity of the

younger sister, which ripened into bitterness—affecting her bones and paralyzing her.
When a certain evangelist came to town, her
sin of unforgiveness was recognized and
repented of, and peace was made between the
two sisters. To God be the glory!

Colitis

In the August-September 1981 issue of *Decision* magazine I read the testimony of Chris-
tine Wood, which begins to pinpoint the subject at hand. She wrote that it took a long and
painful bout of colitis to get her still enough
and quiet enough to hear the whisper of God's
love. Sitting quietly by the ocean, watching
the ebb and flow of the waves, she was im-
pressed by the fact that life needs the same
rhythm. Both in our physical and workaday
lives, as well as in our spiritual lives, we need
to stop and rest, to take time to listen, to make
decisions, and to let the love of Jesus over-
whelm us.

Ulcers and Arthritis

Before I write more on this subject of stress
and disease, I'd like to say that I'm no authority on the subject. I have not gone to medical school or even taken a course in medicine,
nor have I ever been more than a patient in a
hospital. I have, however, read many articles
and books on the subject of the physical and
spiritual, which in turn have shed a lot of light
on my own problems.

If I had known or read about these things 30 years ago, I might have been warned. Whether I would have heeded them will never be known. But perhaps because of this chapter someone else will be better informed and will avoid the same consequences.

God forbid that you should live as long as I have and learn so little about the causes of your own distresses.

I've suffered from two major ailments: a peptic ulcer and osteoarthritis. Doing research for this chapter has been like turning on a light for me. I can now look back and see how both of these developed.

The cause: repressing what I felt I ought to do and doing what I was told to do. My employers (superiors or directors) held me back from using the talents God had given me. They stunted my growth and creativity because my ideas were not a part of the program already planned, and thus my ideas could not be considered. Being a woman compounded my dilemma, and I learned very early that this is a man's world.

The remedy came 25 years ago, when I took a step of faith and became a free-lance writer and speaker. I am free to learn more of Jesus my Lord as I continue the adventure of discovering the heights and depths of His love . . . even now as I write my fourteenth book.

However, now that the proclivity is there, any disturbance out of the will of God brings headaches, and I am alerted at once. Like: overbooking myself with speaking engagements, filling my days too full with daily things (such as writing, telephone calls, and exercise), or failing to face up honestly with another person about what irritates me.

My arthritis, as nearly as I can judge, came from a severe and prolonged mental and emotional situation about which I seemed unable (and therefore unwilling) to make a decision . . . until my bones ached and stiffened, and eventually forced me into a wheelchair every time I was in any airport where I had a long distance to walk.

I finally made the decision which brought a total change. That decision, together with the necessary surgery (total new hip and total new knee) have left me with renewed energy to walk and swim without pain. My problem there, along with not making a positive decision, was also one of refusing to take responsibility for the results.

I'd like to say right here that I would not like to make any of my readers feel guilty of some unknown sin if they have arthritis, etc. I am better today because of the wisdom that God gave the doctors also. It is mutual cooperation between myself, God, and the doctors.

Here are a few Scriptures and lessons I learned.

1. I cried to the Lord and He answered me (Psalm 107).
2. I sought counsel. God gave me a spiritual guide who had wisdom to guide me, and who helped me locate the cause of my distress, and who is still available (Proverbs 11:14; 13:10; 19:20).

3. I found that character is formed and tempered by stress and trials when my heart is set before the Lord as honestly as I am able to do (Romans 5:3-5; 8:28).
4. I've learned to be gentle with others, and not judge them too harshly, knowing that God puts up with a lot even from His servants whom He uses. I pray for those who minister to others.
5. I've learned to be gentle with myself, too. As I judge others, so will I be judged. As I love myself I will be able to love the unlovable (as I see it) in others.
6. I've learned the power of positive affirmations.

Skin Rash for 13 Years

Several years ago I was holding meetings in Texas, and one night after I spoke on confession and its results, a young woman came to me holding out her wrist and asking me to pray that the rash be healed, since no medicine or ointment seemed to help.

"How long have you had this rash?"

"Twelve years," was her answer.

I prayed that the mercy and loving-kindness of Jesus, and His healing hands, would be upon her wrist and upon her spirit, that the source (whatever it was) might be removed as well as the symptoms. There were tears in her eyes as the prayer was over.

A few moments after that, someone called my attention to two women weepng on each other's shoulder. Going over to them, I put an arm around each; one of them was the woman I had just prayed with. She looked up, wiped her eyes, and introduced me to her older sister.

"We haven't spoken to each other for 13 years, and now God has forgiven us and we have forgiven each other."

Then she told me the story. On their mother's deathbed the older sister had promised to love and protect her younger sister. When that sister announced her engagement, the older sister objected strenuously, sure that such a union would ruin her life. But the younger sister was in love and proceeded with her plans. Finally the older sister threatened, "If you marry him, I'll never speak to you again as long as I live."

Thank God for His healing and reconciling power in the name of Jesus Christ!

Daily Frustrations

The following almost-unbelievable list of things happened to a young priest who loves Jesus and who prays for me. All of this happened in only two months.

1. Some people (for whatever reason) tried to stop my ordination, but praise God, they were unable to.
2. A great misunderstanding occurred between the pastor and myself. He has an incurable disease which affects him and makes it difficult for him to work with others.

3. My house has been broken into twice.
4. My house almost burned down two weeks ago.
5. I went to a conference, was served bad meat, and was poisoned. I had to go to a hospital.
6. I had a minor auto accident.
7. I had my wallet lifted.
8. My dog is sick.
9. Now my car is in the garage for two weeks, and the same "bug" is afflicting me as when I was in the hospital.

All this plus a few other minor problems seem so large that all I want to do is sleep to escape. Some of the physical problems resulting from nurturing this inner anger have been: headaches, dizziness, chest pains, and stomach problems. I know the cause and I know the reasons, but somehow and for some reason I haven't had the energy to do anything about it.

I believe in Jesus Christ and the great love He has for me, and I love Him with all my heart, all my soul, and all my strength. After reflecting on the valley of despair into which I had descended, I made a few decisions and carried them out:

1. Confession. I asked for forgiveness for the anxiety, fear, and anger that I carried.
2. I confronted the issues. I am either a victim or a victor, and I choose the latter.
3. I established a trust level with the elder

pastor, and we are now on a plane where we can freely discuss and pray together.

4. I practiced the "groaning exercise" and found that it works. It is a good antidote for emotional pain.[1]

5. I've learned to direct my frustration or anger not at the circumstance, but to get in tune with my own feelings and deal with them.

The Breakdown from Then Until Now

Today, as in Old Testament times, the breakdown comes when we begin to worship false gods (which are idols) in order to satisfy our needs or desires to follow the crowd. Our "right to ourselves" seems logical, and we are caught up in securing position, wealth, sex, comfort, houses, lands, education, or whatever it is that money or influence can procure.

The Prophet Ezekiel prophesied against the children of Israel in Ezekiel chapters 33 to 35 because of their idolatry, which he labeled "spiritual adultery." Almost every sin—personal, social, or political—is found in those chapters, yet God, for His holy name's sake and the great loving-kindness He had for His people, gave them hope. In chapters 36 and 37 He promised to make those dead bones live

---

[1]The groaning exercise: Get alone somewhere, preferably lying down, and groan aloud with every breath you exhale. *Prevention* magazine had an article on this a few months ago, and I shared it with my friend. They suggest groaning for 20 minutes, but when I tried it in a time of need, I was okay in five minutes.

again, and to give them a new heart and a new spirit and to cleanse them from all uncleanness.

We even make idols of our God-given talents or abilities, which push Him out of the picture, such as making friends, raising a family, making money to further God's work, writing, music, art, education, travel, etc. More trouble arises because when we break the first commandment, we soon break the second. Or . . . which do we break first?

Jesus' Knowledge of Our Minds

Loving the Lord our God is still the only answer, for when we are convinced that God loves us unconditionally, that His love is eternal, we can love ourselves. Then it is possible to love our neighbors.

Jesus knew this, and on one occasion He had courage to deal with the root-problem before He dealt with the illness which affected the body. He was criticized for this by the religious authorities of His day because they did not know who He was or what power He possessed. They had no idea of His purpose or ministry on earth, nor did they know the delicate balance between body, mind, and spirit.

Four men came bringing a paralyzed friend (Mark 2:1-12) to Jesus, and because of the crowd in and around the house, they finally got up on the roof, removed some of the tiles, and let the man down through the ceiling right in front of Jesus. Jesus saw *their faith* and said to the paralytic, "My son, your sins are forgiven."

That set up quite a reaction. If I had been one of the four people holding the ropes on that stretcher, I probably would have called down, "But, Master, we want You to heal *his body*." The reaction of the religious elite was only in their minds: "This is blasphemy! Who can forgive sins but God alone?"

Jesus read their minds immediately. "Why do you question thus in your hearts? Which is easier to say to the paralytic, 'Your sins are forgiven' or to say, 'Rise, take up your pallet and walk'? But that you may know that the Son of man has authority on earth to forgive sins"—he said to the paralytic—"I say to you, rise, take up your pallet and go home."

The truth was that one was as easy for Jesus to do or say as the other. They could do neither, and were alarmed and perplexed by the power He possessed. While the common people glorified God, the religious authorities went away still questioning what they heard rather than what they saw. In the very next healing episode of Jesus, recorded in Mark 3:1-6, they again watched a healing take place, this time on the Sabbath, which added to their condemnation of this Man. He was dangerous —dangerous enough to be destroyed. So they "went out and immediately held counsel with the Herodians [the political power of Rome] against him, how to destroy him" (Mark 3:6).

Jesus' Purpose on Earth

In spite of their condemnation, Jesus continued His ministry of healing the body and the spirit, as well as eating and drinking with sinners, though He knew He was being watched. His answer was:

> Those who are well have no need of a physician, but those who are sick; I came not to call the righteous, but sinners (Mark 2:17).

> I am the good shepherd. . . . I came that they [my sheep] may have life, and have it abundantly (John 10:11,10).

> The Spirit of the Lord is upon me, because he has anointed me to preach good news to the poor. He has sent me to proclaim release to the captives and recovering of sight to the blind, to set at liberty those who are oppressed, to proclaim the acceptable year of the Lord (Luke 4:18,19; Isaiah 61:1,2).

Questions About Illness

Jesus, who saw the questioning in the minds of those who watched Him that day, also knew the total condition of the paralyzed man before Him. Apparently He knew there was a grievous sin which was eating into his spirit and which finally affected his body. So in compassion He first dealt with the cause (his sin) and then with the symptom (his paralysis). In other healings, Jesus attributed some illness from Satan, and with authority cast him out, making the person whole.

Is all paralysis caused by sin?

Is all sickness and illness caused by sin or Satan?

When Adam and Eve sinned, the perfection of earth was marred, and death, sin, and disease came upon us all. The second Adam, Jesus Christ, Himself became the remedy and in a sense "took the rap" for us all. It took the great mind and spirit of the Apostle Paul in Romans chapter 5 to bring us the meaning of the first and second Adam. Be sure to read Romans 4:17 and 1 Peter 2:24,25.

Today there are many people who take both sides of this question. Some teach that all illness is in the mind; others teach that illness needs divine deliverance from Satan. The truth lies in discernment, a gift of the Holy Spirit (1 Corinthians 12:10). There are epidemics, accidents, and events beyond our control which bring out latent physical tendencies in our bodies.

Much progress has been made in the science of the mind, and while the Bible is not a science textbook, the lists of sins to avoid bring certain results within us and around us which can be effectively dealt with in prayer, in confession, and in receiving forgiveness. Many of our ailments are self-induced, because we fail to recognize their source, or seem unable or unwilling to face them.

We are wonderfully and fearfully made, and without the healing touch of our Saviour and Creator, how helpless we are!

With God all things are possible, and meditation in the presence of the Lord our God is the greatest resource open to us all. Let Him speak to you through His Word. Trust Him for guidance and enlightenment as soon as you are aware of stress in your life. It could be as simple as taking a break and breathing deeply. Later in this book I'll share with you how I combine *The Jesus Prayer* with deep breathing.

> Always remember what I tell you to do. My teaching will give you a long and prosperous life. ... Tie them around your neck; write them on your heart. If you do this, both God and man will be pleased with you. Trust in the Lord with all your heart. Never rely on what you think you know. Remember the Lord in everything you do, and he will show you the right way. Never let yourself think you are wiser than you are; simply obey the Lord and refuse to do wrong. If you do, it will be like good medicine, healing your wounds and easing your pains (Proverbs 3:1-8 TEV).

Review

Group Sharing

1. There are at least ten ways suggested in this chapter to handle stress positively. Find them.
2. When is stress good? When is it harmful?

3. What does facing "the negatives before the positives" mean?
4. Homework: Examine your own past history. Ask the Lord to help you locate your "negatives" so you can cooperate mentally and spiritually to obey Him.

Group Activity

1. In small groups (of two or three, so people can pray without fear), ask your loving Lord to reveal causes of distress, and ask for honesty to name them.
2. Listen carefully to yourself and to each other. Pray for courage to make the next necessary decision.

> Fear not, for I am with you;
> be not dismayed, for I am your God;
> I will strengthen you, I will help you,
> I will uphold you with my
> victorious right hand (Isaiah 41:10).

Practical Ways to Handle Stress

Successfully handling stress promotes good health and wholeness. In the varied stories of stress diseases in this chapter, you will find a good list of things to get started on.

1. Take time to be with your Lord—to listen, to worship, to meditate, to lay out your plans before Him. This will clear your thinking, relieve your anxiety, and help you to relax and sleep.

2. Learn to say no and not feel guilty. Set your priorities, make wise decisions, and trust God to help you.
3. Confession, absolution, and restitution are essential. Forgive yourself, your sister, your mother, or any other offending party.
4. Find a wise spiritual counselor.
5. Learn to live in the present. Forget the past, and trust God with the future.
6. Learn to laugh at yourself. Take time to play games with friends or to take a day off. Cultivate some pastime or skill which you enjoy.
7. Feed on the promises given in the Bible. Write them out and memorize them (Romans 8:26-39; 2 Corinthians 4:7-18; plus many others that you will find for yourself).

Meditation for Chapter 9

Come, my soul, thy suit prepare:
   Jesus loves to answer prayer;
He Himself has bid thee pray,
   Therefore will not say thee nay.

Thou art coming to a King;
   Large petitions with thee bring;
For His grace and power are such,
   None can ever ask too much.

                            —John Newton

CHAPTER 9

Benefits of a Prayer Partner

Ever since Mildred Rice (my fellow missionary in China) and I discovered the simplicity and power in conversational (or dialogue) prayer that memorable day in Peking, I have been a firm believer in praying together.

I must tell you honestly that I haven't always had a definite prayer partner, but I have always been free to ask for prayers for myself, and others have asked me to pray for them. That is one of the first steps to freedom in audible prayer for those whose hearts long for a prayer partner.

How does one find a prayer partner?

You ask the Lord God to give you one.

Then you keep your eyes open to see how He is going to answer that prayer. You also keep the ears of your heart open to hear what that inner voice tells you. In my prayer workshops when I speak on this subject, I call for a time of silent prayer when each person present asks for a name. When the time is over and I ask how many people had definite names given to them, there are hands raised or broad smiles. If those persons are not present, I suggest that they go home and share with them and invite them to be their prayer partner. It works every time.

Fear of Praying Aloud?

Is it necessary to pray with someone else? Didn't Jesus say to go into your closet and pray? Yes, and that is a precious promise too, and needs our obedience. But in that same context He also rebuked those who made long prayers in public to be seen of men.

My experience in prayer workshops has been that those who have reservations about praying aloud are some of God's needing-to-be-unbound children. Their fears are not from the Lord (God has not given us the spirit of fear—2 Timothy 1:7 KJV). Here are a few fears which you can face and let go, and my prayers join yours.

1. Fear of being emotional? God made tears for a release. Love is an emotion that needs to be expressed. Tears are liquid love.
2. Fear of nothing to say? Make your prayers short and to the point. Say what the Spirit puts into your heart.
3. Somebody else already said it? That is agreement, so be sure and say, "Thank You, Lord, for that prayer which You also gave me." Be encouraged, not discouraged.
4. You think others pray better than you do? Again I say: short prayers, thanks, agreement: "Thank You, Lord," or, "I agree with that prayer."

First Lesson in Prayer

I speak in many liturgical churches, and I find many people who are well-acquainted with the liturgy but hesitant to start praying together. Let me share an outline I use which has been helpful:

1. *Be a child in Jesus' presence.* That means simplicity and honesty, not trying to impress anybody.
2. *Ask for only one specific thing at a time.* Let your partner agree, or pray some more on that subject. When you can give thanks, it is time to introduce a new subject.
3. *Ask a NOW prayer.* This means something which the Lord can do to begin to answer your prayers. (See next chapter.)

Don't just pray, "Lord, bless all the people who need You in Africa." I call that a blanket prayer, and you'll never know when you get an answer. Instead, pray for someone you know there, or some situation you know about.

Blind Bartimaeus, in answer to Jesus' invitation, "What do you want me to do for you?" answered with a NOW prayer: "Master, let me receive my sight." Jesus told him that *his faith* made him well. He asked for a specific thing, in a short prayer, in the presence of Jesus, and he got his answer.

That is an easily remembered pattern, and it works.

The Special Promise

Our Lord has given a very special promise for two who agree and ask for anything in His presence. To agree means to be in harmony with. In His presence also means "in His name" and "in His will."

Most believers know these verses:

> I say to you, if two of you agree on earth about anything they ask, it will be done for them by my Father in heaven. For where two or three are gathered in my name, there am I in the midst of them.

These words are found in Matthew chapter 18, verses 19 and 20. Do you know the verse which just precedes these? That is a very important verse, for it gives us the clue about what we are to do when we agree in prayer for something or someone.

We are given two verbs which we ought to begin to use, as we are led by the Spirit, instead of the word *bless.* They are *binding* and *loosing.* Have you ever noticed how believers overwork the word *bless?* Actually, it keeps us from asking anything definite, for it is easier and simpler to say "Lord, bless my sister" than it is to quietly wait in prayer until we find what the Spirit would like to do for that sister, such as, "Lord, may my sister be aware of Your love and Your presence in a special way today. Bind any depression which may come to her today. Loose in her a spirit of thankfulness."

Here is that verse 18 from Matthew chapter 18:

> Truly I say to you, whatever you bind on earth shall be bound in heaven,

and whatever you loose on earth shall
be loosed in heaven.

Just what it means to loose and to bind we
will examine in the next chapter, but because
Jesus said it, I believe there is more power in
prayers which follow His instructions.

There Is Work to Be Done

First of all, let us remind ourselves that
when we pray alone it is largely devotional,
but we are also here to do business with our
Lord. When we pray with our partner, we are
there to make ourselves available to the Lord
our God to participate in whatever work He
has in mind. Too many times we come and in-
form Him of what He already knows, and we
do not expect anything more than "a blessing"
from Him. Well, let us be thankful for blessings, but there is work to be done also, and
Jesus told His disciples (including us):

> Truly, truly, I say to you, he who
> believes in me will also do the works
> that I do; and greater works than
> these will he do, because I go to the
> Father. Whatever you ask in my
> name, I will do it, that the Father may
> be glorified in the Son; if you ask
> anything in my name, I will do it
> (John 14:12-14).

My greatest answers to prayer come when
two or more of us are praying together in His

presence, which means in His name. "In His name" is not just a phrase tacked to the end of our prayers; praying in Jesus' name means praying in His presence, for He is the third Person present when two human beings pray.

My Own Prayer Partners

Through my years of ministry to others, the Lord has given me various persons to pray with, but because of my heavy traveling schedule we had no regular times to meet. Sometimes we prayed over the telephone, and sometimes requests came and went in letters. However, the more I have observed what happens when people pray, and the more I have observed the needs of the church at large, the more convinced I am that God honors two people praying together. They are a power unit.

Think what it would mean to your pastor in his ministry as he looked over the congregation and saw two-by-two power units among his parishioners with whom he knew he could share the many burdens he carries, and who were praying quietly even during worship services.

When I moved to California, eight years ago, I hoped for a less strenuous schedule, but I can't say I found it. However, I did find two things for which I had definitely prayed—a home church and a resident prayer partner.

> . . . to him who by the power at work
> within us is able to do far more abun-
> dantly than all that we ask or think,
> to him be glory in the church and in

> Christ Jesus to all generations, for
> ever and ever. Amen (Ephesians
> 3:20,21).

Actually, there are two churches where I feel at home, and where people love and pray for me—St. James Episcopal in Newport Beach and Emmanual Episcopal in Fullerton.

Here's how God answered both those requests. Betty Connelly invited me to become a member of St. James in Newport Beach, and she soon became a valued friend and frequent prayer partner, as well as a coleader in workshops. The Rev. Paul Edwards of Emmanuel invited me to hold a prayer workshop for his people, and out of that came many good things, including the love and prayers of that church and Fr. Paul himself is my spiritual advisor.

Then there is Frances Forkish, whom God sent in answer to our prayers to become my helper, part-time secretary, and prayer partner. Frances and John had come from Maryland, seeking a church home and that's how our contact began. She has become a valued friend and assistant.

Added to these blessings is a list of more than 30 prayer partners with whom I share my speaking and writing schedules, and they have certain days on which each partner prays especially for me.

The "more abundant" answer for which I thank God is a Friday morning prayer group which meets right here in Laguna Hills, in the home of Nellie Sillers. Nellie Sillers and Florence Norton followed me around to six of my talks on prayer, and soon afterward I heard that Nellie had started a group in her home using conversational prayer. I called on the telephone to congratulate them, and was promptly invited to attend. I've been going ever since, and I praise God for the love and prayer support which we give to each other.

Once a day on the telephone, Nellie and I exchange prayer requests. Writing this book has been a daily subject for prayer, and when I feel enemy opposition regarding time or subject, I call her, and immediately she prays a NOW prayer right on the wire, and I get back to work again. She prays that interruptions will be at a minimum and that I will have a clear mind to receive the guidance of the Spirit as I write.

The result has been that this is one of the easiest books I've written. When I sit down to write, the material just flows out of my fingers to the typewriter (with not too many corrections). All praise be to our God who answers prayers!

Nellie keeps a notebook and writes down daily requests, which we then share with the Friday group. Always part of our meeting includes giving each person an opportunity to tell how God has worked personally in answering prayer during the past week. Here are some things which encourage us, and I hope will help motivate you as God leads you.

General Subjects for Our Support-Group

1. We pray for each person present.

2. We ask each person for a personal request and pray for each request as it is given.
3. We pray for a list of "lingering ill" geriatrics from our churches.
4. We pray for Rosalind's speaking engagements, travel safety, and anointing.
5. We pray for our nation, our President, our congressmen, and local problems as they arise.
6. We pray for missions and missionaries.
7. We pray for friends and relatives who need Christ.

The number of specific persons prayed for in a particular one-month period ranged from 34 to 44. During a two-week period this summer we prayed for 54 people.

Just to give you an idea of some of those requests and answers, here are a few:

For Rosalind:

1. Ten days with Episcopal Diocese of South Dakota.
   Answer: Renewal uniting Indians and Caucasians through the ministry of Cursillos prepared the way for effective workshops on prayer in four cities.
2. Three days sponsored by Diocesan Commission on Renewal and Evangelism in Boston.
   Answer: Thank God for the privilege of taking part in the renewal going on there.
3. Prayer for preparation for the 30 speaking engagements of 1981 as they come due.

Several other definite answers to prayer will be shared in the next chapter, where we describe the practice of *holding-prayer,* which is closely related to faith-sized prayers.

Among the many answers we had were the following: restored faith and trust, ability to pray aloud, lost articles found, a successful art exhibit, solution of mental and spiritual problems, and answers to physical health problems.

Principles We Follow

1. Short prayers (anyone is able to add more).
2. Healing of the person's spirit first, as we believe that spiritual healing comes before physical.
3. Terminal illness: that God in mercy will take the person quickly and without pain.
4. Laying on of hands for each other, and by proxy.
5. Praying for long lists of those we do not know. One person reads the name: Sally Jones. All of us respond: God bless Sally. Until the list is covered.

We ask for guidance as to how long each person remains on our list.

Benefits of Praying Together

In closing this chapter, here is a brief outline

of this subject taken from my book *Praying Together.*[1]

1. Answers are promised to those who agree.
2. We really get to know other people.
3. We learn to accept ourselves.
4. We find joy and release in praying together.
5. Nominal church members start praying and find Christ real in their lives for the first time.
6. We are alerted in times of crisis.
7. We have a new awareness of God's presence.
8. God's love is given to us and through us.

Our Circle of Love

Opening our meeting: We stand in a circle with hands crossed and grasping the hand of the person next to us. We give sentences of thanks and praise for Jesus' presence with us, and for other blessings. Then we sit down, read some Scripture, and do the things outlined in this chapter.

Closing our meeting: We stand in a circle of love once more, repeating together the Lord's Prayer and the Mizpah. Sometimes we sing a song or a chorus.

We come away with joy and gladness in our hearts, and with thanks to God for such a loving, caring, praying support-group.

---

[1]Rosalind Rinker, *Praying Together*, Chapter 7 (Zondervan, 1968).

Review

Group Sharing

1. Share any fears you may still have on praying aloud. Describing the fears aloud helps make them powerless.
2. Memorize the three steps in *First Lessons on Prayer*. Have you tried them yet? With whom?
3. Discuss the words "bless," "find," "loose," and how they are misused, and how Jesus taught us to use them.

Group Activity

1. Share how you found your prayer partner, and pray with those in your group who have not yet found one.
2. If you have not already done so, copy and memorize the special prayer promises found in Matthew 18:18-20. Carry the paper (or card) around with you and repeat these promises until they are a part of you.

Meditation for Chapter 10

Thine arm, O Lord, in days of old
  Was strong to heal and save;
It triumphed o'er disease and death,
  O'er darkness and the grave.
To thee they went—the blind, the dumb,
  The palsied and the lame,
The leper with his tainted life,
  The sick with fevered frame.

And lo! thy touch brought life and health,
  Gave speech, and strength, and sight;
And youth renewed and frenzy calmed
  Owned thee, the Lord of light.
And now, O Lord, be near to bless,
  As by Gennesaret's shore.

Be thou our great deliverer still,
  Be Lord of life and death;
Restore and quicken, soothe and bless,
  With thine almighty breath;
To hands that work and eyes that see,
  Give wisdom's heavenly lore,
That whole and sick, and weak and strong,
  May praise thee evermore.

                    —E. H. Plumtre

CHAPTER 10

The Prayer of Faith-Sized Requests

What is a faith-sized request?

It is a prayer which uses the faith you now have to reach out step by step in more faith as you prove God's faithfulness and see the answers come to pass.

A faith-sized request is just the right "believing" size for what you really believe that God can do. This does not limit Him, but lets your faith grow so you can ask for greater things.

There are several lessons for us in the promise that Jesus gave us in Mark 11:22-25:

> Have faith in God. Truly I say to you, whoever says to this mountain, "Be taken up and cast into the sea," and does not doubt in his heart, but believes that what he says will come to pass, it will be done for him. Therefore I tell you, whatever you ask in prayer, believe that you receive it, and you will. And whenever you stand praying, forgive, if you have anything against anyone; so that your Father also who is in heaven may forgive you your trespasses.

Basic Lessons in Faith

1. Believe what you are saying, when you ask for something.

2. Believe that with God nothing is impossible.
3. To believe in your heart means to concentrate on the answer, not on the problem.
4. Do not concentrate on how big the mountain before you is; instead, visualize how big a splash it makes when it falls into the sea! Plus, see that open road to the goal awaiting you.
5. Remember, "Faith comes from what is heard, and what is heard comes by the preaching of Christ" (Romans 10:17).

The youth director of our church told me that his teenagers like word studies. For instance, *faith.* They'll look up all the references found in their concordances, and try to organize them and pray over them. Jesus spoke of people with no faith, little faith, and great faith.

Visualize Your Request

Our most urgent prayers are for our own health or for the health and salvation of our loved ones. Why do so many of these prayers take so long to answer?

We know when we pray for good health that this is the will of the Lord. When we pray for our loved ones to find Christ, that is in the will of the Lord also.

Let's look at two people who came to Jesus for healing and found it immediately. Both overcame obstacles to be face-to-face with Jesus. First, blind Bartimaeus (Mark 10:46-52) asked only once for himself, while the second person, the Canaanite woman (Matthew 15:21-28), asked many times for her daughter. I'm sure both of these people *saw that healing already done in their minds,* and that is what triggered their courage in asking.

The blind man had nothing but time on his hands—time to listen to reports about the Man who healed others, time to think about what could happen to him if Jesus ever came out of that Jericho gate, time to think about what he would do in that case.

We call that *expectation.* Expectation is like visualization—he saw and imagined what it would be like after Jesus gave him his sight again. Would you like to have faith like this? Then follow his example until you finally are in the presence of Jesus.

Expectation is also the mother of hope. The Canaanite woman surely visualized her daughter made whole, and that gave her courage to approach Jesus even when she had no right to do so. He commended her for her great faith, and she got her answer. So did Bartimaeus.

When we pray for our loved ones, we must visualize their faces as they will be after Jesus comes into their hearts. How many of us are guilty of only informing God of all the things wrong about that person which need to be changed! That is looking at the mountain itself instead of having courage to say "Drop into the sea!" In our mind's eye we must see the changed faces because the hearts are changed.

Praying in the Will of God

When we pray for healing we must remember that Jesus willed that people should be made whole.

His touch brought healing.

His very word brought wholeness.

His presence brought expectation, hope, and faith.

Reports about Him brought hope to the hopeless.

Today we pray for God to heal us, or we pray for others to be healed. Yet all are not healed. God takes us home in His own time, and usually it is not "our time." Why more people are not healed is a question I can't answer for you.

I do know that when I pray for a sick person who has requested prayer, I quietly ask God to guide me in whatever I ask.

Praying for the Terminally Ill

I live in a retirement center because it offers more security (I travel a great deal) and a large pool which I need for exercise. We have a Friday morning prayer meeting here, and usually our list of terminally ill people is a long one. We have often remarked that it seems more painful to get out of this world than it is to get into it!

Many of these people ask us to pray that God will take them quickly, and He does. My own dear mother prayed that when her time came, God would take her quickly so that the money could go to foreign missions instead of toward a huge medical bill. That was a real prayer of faith, because it happened just like that.

Agnes Sanford taught me (from her books) to wait silently first, when asked to pray, and to lay hands of faith on the sick people. I know that the power and healing come from Jesus Christ, who is our risen Healer, but He uses you and me as instruments and wants us to ask Him for healing (Luke 11:1-13).

If It Be Thy Will

I once put this phrase at the end of everything I asked just in case I was out of divine order. Now I know that this is a cop-out, a failure to wait upon the Lord until I know what His will is.

This is where faith-sized requests come in. I've learned to start with something I can believe, and when that happens, I go on to the next thing as it is shown to me.

To ask the Lord for something but then add "If it be Thy will" is like blowing a circuit. We need to plug into the power and find the will of God for what we ask. Then we have the faith which laughs at impossibilities!

The Prayer of Faith

My sister, Denise Adler of Seattle, plugged into that power line and found the will of God regarding the melanoma (tumor) on her face. She knew right from the first that God was going to heal her by whatever means He chose.

She told me that in order to build her faith, she looked up all the Bible references she could find on healing and wrote them on cards. "I quoted them, I memorized them, I read them night and day, when I couldn't sleep, anywhere I was. This helped my faith to grow."

During six surgeries she announced with quietness and confidence that God was going to heal her as if it were a completed fact. She told the specialists, the surgeon, the nurses, and all her friends. We marveled at the strength of her faith. The prognosis for this kind of cancer is eventually terminal, but she refused to think negative thoughts. At each surgery she took another step of faith.

Then a new treatment was brought over by two doctors from Sweden called B.C.G. it was to be tried out at the clinic on only three persons, and Denise was one of them.

The amazing results brought much glory to the name of Jesus Christ and thanksgiving from all her loved ones as we witnessed her complete healing over a period of four years. This story can readily be broken into faith-sized requests during that time.

The Lord has had His hand on Denise for some years now, building trust and achieving faith. She was the teaching leader for Seattle's Bible Study Fellowship for seven years, and the class divided every time it reached a membership of 500 (and spread to adjoining cities). After she left on account of illness, at the request of friends she started a small group which met and grew until they were forced to move into John Knox Presbyterian Church.

Not only did she teach those classes, but her studies were carried into many churches and lands by the women, until finally Tyndale Publishing House started publishing the studies. The story of her healing has circulated and encouraged other women to find the will of God and pray the prayer of faith.

When Jesus' disciples asked why they couldn't cast out the disease causing epilepsy, He replied, "Because of your little faith. For truly I say to you, if you have faith as a grain of mustard seed, you will say to this mountain, 'Move hence to yonder place,' and it will move; and nothing will be impossible to you" (Matthew 17:20,21).

On other occasions Jesus said, "What is impossible with men is possible with God" (Luke 18:27). "All things are possible to him who believes" (Mark 9:23).

The Stairway of Faith-Sized Requests

Not all of us know the will of God as quickly or as strongly as Denise did in that last story. So we take as much as we can believe, and we go on from there. Let me illustrate the prayer of faith by using a flight of stairs, with each step representing one faith-sized request which we can believe before we go on to another request.

You never take a whole flight in one single stride, but in a series of steps. Look back on some answer to prayer you have had, and perhaps you can trace the steps you took.

I remember hearing a woman pray for her daughter-in-law to accept Christ as Saviour. It's like she's at the bottom of the stairs and her answer is at the top. I asked her how long she had been making this request, and she told me eight years. When I asked if she saw any signs of the answer, tears came, and I found that she not only opposed the wedding but was not welcome in that home (and there were four grandchildren).

She needed to get on that first step and admit her lack of love. The second step: confessing it to the Lord and receiving forgiveness. Then she would be free to pray and act accordingly. There could be more steps, too, such as listening creatively to God's voice on just when and how to show that love.

Five Questions People Always Ask

The subjects which have just been considered always find some people with more questions, so here they are if you need them.

1. *If we ask more than once, is our faith lacking?*
    Most of the people who asked Jesus to heal them in New Testament days asked only once. But twice Jesus told parables about those who persisted: 1) the Canaanite woman (Matthew 15:21-28) who persisted was complimented by Jesus: "O woman, great is your faith! Be it done for you as you desire." And her daughter was healed instantly, even though the mother was not present; 2) the midnight disturber who in-

sisted on getting bread for a friend was commended because he was not ashamed to keep on asking (Luke 11:5-13). Jesus taught, *Ask, seek, and knock,* which meant, *Don't give up.* Yes, you can ask more than once.

2. *Is it necessary for "laying on of hands" for the prayer of healing?*

Jesus usually laid hands on those He healed. Yet twice He healed those who were not even in His presence, when He saw the faith of those asking: 1) the story above, about the Canaanite woman's daughter; and 2) the centurion's servant (Matthew 8:5-13). Jesus commended this man for his great faith and marveled that He had so seldom seen it. The young church in the Acts of the Apostles practiced "laying on of hands" (Acts 8:18; 1 Timothy 4:14; James 5:14). Therefore, it is not essential, but touching is a means of identifying with another person in the love of God as we pray for each other.

3. *In praying the prayer of faith, is it necessary always to pray with another person or to have someone agree with you?*

No, it is not. Look at Abraham. God spoke to him when there was no Bible to read and no one to consult with. He obeyed, left his home for an unknown country, and was even ready to sacrifice Isaac.

Then there is Noah, who amid the ridicule of neighbors built a ship on dry land because God told him to.

And Joshua—can you imagine him consulting with his warriors about marching around Jericho with torches and shouts?

And Daniel. And the Apostle Paul at the time of his conversion.

However, I believe that there is more prayer-power generated when two people pray, because Jesus said so (Matthew 18:18-20). The Holy Spirit guides us and is faithful to help us do the will of God without fear.

4. *What do you think about fasting in order to get your prayers answered?*
I believe it is effective, because Jesus taught it (Mark 9:14-29).

When the disciples could not cast out the dumb spirit, the father cried to Jesus, "I believe; help Thou mine unbelief." After the healing, the disciples asked why they could not do that, and Jesus replied, "This kind can come forth by nothing but by prayer and fasting."

Fasting is almost a lost art today. Personally, I'll admit I need to know more about it. I do know that when God speaks and people obey, He blesses them.

5. *Didn't Jesus pray "If it be Thy will?" Then why can't we pray this when we are asking for something?*
Jesus *knew* His Father's will. He came to give His life, to lay it down, to die on the cross. But He also knew that He would rise again. His prayer in Gethsemane, "not my will but thine be done" (Luke 22:42), was not one of fear, or of questioning His Father's will, or of trying to change it, but

of His holy Person drawing back from the horrors of the cross awaiting Him. Our problem is not the will of God. It is our lack of faith, our failure to wait in prayer until we know God's will. He waits to speak to us, to guide and direct us. In our immaturity and impatience we tack that phrase on the end of our prayers like a safety clause—as if God would ever do anything out of His will!

The Faith-Sized Prayers of Intercession

This chapter would not be complete unless we summarized these prayers, and then I want to share with you one of the important answers God gave me this past year when I prayed for a friend in her midnight hour which illustrates many of the prayers listed.

Here is a summary of the kinds of prayers we need to be aware of and to use in our interceding for others:

1. *The Prayer of Faith,* which means prayer in the name of Jesus and prayer in the will of God (Acts 3:6,16).
2. *The Closet Prayer,* alone with your Lord (Matthew 6:6).
3. *The Forgiving Prayer* (forgiveness for yourself and in regard to your brother or sister).
4. *The Agreeing Prayer,* with two or three or more people (Matthew 18:19,20).
5. *The Healing Prayer* (James 5;13-16).
6. *The Holding Prayer*—persistent, not giving up, continuing to pray until the answer

comes (Matthew 15:21-28; Luke 11:5-13).

7. *The Prayer of Authority* (Matthew 18:18): binding the enemy and loosing the captive in the name of Jesus.

8. *The Prayer of Deliverance*, which should be carefully looked into, and given by someone with authority and the special gift for this kind of prayer.

9. *The Prayers of Meditation and Contemplation.*

10. *The Prayers of Praise and Thanksgiving.*

The Prayer of Binding and Loosing

For many years I quoted Matthew 18:19,20, until one day the Holy Spirit awakened me to verse 18 and to that whole chapter, which is on the failure of brothers to forgive and to love one another. The resulting suffering is sometimes almost more than can be borne, and especially alone.

There is power generated when two people agree and pray together, for our risen Lord has promised to be right there with them. He wants to set His children free, but He apparently needs our cooperation, for He has conquered our archenemy, Satan, who still appears as an angel of light or as a roaring lion, seeking whom he can devour.

God gave me an opportunity to minister like this to one of His children suffering from needless pain which might have been avoided if other Christian brothers had walked in guidance.

Fourteen years ago I lived in Honolulu for

several years, and for only three months had a daily radio program on which I seemed able to talk about only one subject: the unconditional love of God through Jesus Christ for everyone regardless of performance—love based on His eternal character, not on our ups and downs, but on the real Personage within each of us. Among the fan letters I received were several from Crying Wind, a young woman married to a G.I., to whom that message came like a cool breeze in a desert land. We have corresponded ever since.

I was delighted beyond measure when she wrote her first book, *Crying Wind*, and then her second, *My Searching Heart* (1979). Her struggle from one culture (Navajo) to another (Christian), her worship of the wind, her tenacity to keep going, and the final publishing of her story and how Jesus found her have brought many of Indian heritage to Christ, as well as many Caucasians who have read her books.

Then the blow fell! She was blacklisted as having misrepresented her story. No more books for anybody.

Her letters to me were full of unspeakable pain. She was desperate beyond all comfort. Did Christians do things like this? Why should she live any longer? Didn't God care either? Why did this happen?

Finally I got the whole story. An uncle whom she wrote about in her second book was goaded by some well-meaning friend to ask for a large portion of her royalties. She explained why she couldn't give him that amount. For the first time in their married lives, she and Don and their four children had purchased a home of their own, with new furnishings, and all on monthly payments. They were also saving some for the children's education.

He was not only offended, but he was angry and left muttering that he'd fix her. He did. He went to the publisher and said that Crying Wind had told them a pack of lies in her books. Without a thorough investigation, the publishers acted, destroying the books.

So now what? They lost the house and the furnishings, and they lived on "care" packages from the church, after paying what they owed. I did the best I could, writing her to have courage, to read David's Psalms of lament in times of suffering, that God would vindicate her and that someday she could write about it. That seemed small comfort.

Then I took it to our Friday morning prayer group, and together we claimed the *binding* of Satan, who was oppressing this child of God, and claimed that Christ's victory would loose her and vindicate her.

One day the Lord spoke to me so plainly that I had to act. Why didn't I do something about it? Why didn't I help her find another publisher? I called my longtime friend Bob Hawkins and told him the story. He said, "Ros, find a bigger publisher than I am: I've only been in this a few years." I tried the two publishers who print my books, with telephone calls right to the top, and was told to send copies of her book.

More than a month passed with no word from anywhere. We kept praying and kept reminding the Lord of His promise, and that those two books be unbound and loosed to give blessing and salvation.

This is a story that has long needed to be told, and I'm glad I can tell it in the context of answered prayer.

One day the telephone rang, and Bob Hawkins wanted Crying Wind's telephone number. He wanted to publish her books! What had happened? He had attended a conference of some kind and had met a knowledgeable person concerning the true story about her books. Crying Wind felt that there had been a great misunderstanding about her books. Bob suggested that the books *Crying Wind* and *My Searching Heart* be called biographical novels.

In less than a month, the presses were running and 60,000 books had been sold. All praise and thanks be to the Lord Jesus, in whose mighty name we had claimed the answer! The books were again in the hands of people who were hungry to know God's ways with His children.

> Therefore I tell you, whatever you ask in prayer, believe that you receive it, and you will (Mark 11:24).

What We Learn from the Prayer of Faith

1. Faith is born first of all from hearing and reading what Jesus can do and has done. Then comes hope and expectation.

2. Those who pray this prayer have time to think about confronting Jesus. They go where He is to be found, where His people are. The mercyseat is always open to us.
3. They only asked one thing. How many things do you ask for at one time? How urgent is that need?
4. They were desperate, and in spite of people who might hinder, they persisted until they got their answer.
5. God was glorified in the healing which resulted.
6. Unanswered prayer is one of God's ways to tell us that we have not sought His specific will, that our faith is not equal to our asking, or that we do not allow Him time to change us or the other person. It could even be that He has something better planned for us.
7. Let us remind ourselves whenever we need to that our faithful Father in heaven knew the answer to our need (problem) long before we even knew there was one.
8. Let us bless His Holy name and lift our hearts and our hands in gratitude and praise. All honor, glory, and blessing be unto the Lamb, for He is worthy!

Review

Group Sharing

1. Name the important steps in the prayer of faith as used in the subtitles in this chapter.

2. Discuss the step which helps you the most.

Group Activity

1. Select three prayer partners for today, and have each one share a long-unanswered prayer.
2. Then pray honestly for yourself first.
3. The other two partners will help you pray the prayer of authority and thanksgiving.
4. Be open to listen creatively as the Holy Spirit reveals any blockage or the next step.

Faith-sized Promise

"Ask, and it will be given you;
    Seek, and you will find;
        Knock, and it will be opened to you.
For everyone who asks receives, and he who seeks finds, and to him who knocks it will be opened. . . . If you . . . know how to give good gifts to your children, how much more will your Father who is in heaven give good things to those who ask Him?" (Matthew 7:7,8,11).

Meditation for Chapter 11

How sweet the name of Jesus sounds
   In a believer's ear!
It soothes his sorrows, heals his wounds,
   And drives away his fear.

It makes the wounded spirit whole,
   And calms the troubled breast;
'Tis manna to the hungry soul,
   And to the weary rest.

Dear Name! The Rock on which I build,
   My Shield and Hiding place,
My never-failing Treasury, filled
   With boundless stores of grace.

Jesus! my Shepherd, Husband, Friend,
   My Prophet, Priest and King;
My Lord, my Life, my Way, my End—
   Accept the praise I bring.

                      —John Newton

CHAPTER 11

The Prayers of Meditation and Worship

The Precious Name of Jesus

From early childhood I remember and often sing an old hymn:

Take the name of Jesus with you,
Child of sorrow and of woe;
It will joy and comfort give you;
Take it, then, where'er you go.
Precious name, O how sweet,
Hope of earth and joy of heaven!

Only the great love and mercy of God who drew us to Himself can account for the reason some of us center on Jesus Christ in our worship, while others center on the Father or the Holy Spirit. I believe that we worship one God who has revealed Himself in these three Persons.

I also believe that when we sing the song of Revelation 5:9-14, we will understand it all.

Worthy art thou to take the scroll and
to open its seals, for thou wast slain
and by thy blood didst ransom men
for God

That same chapter gives us the basis of all prayer. To pray effectively both in our devotional life and in our ministry to others, it is imperative that our faith is firm, solid, and personal regarding Jesus Christ, including His Person and His work on the cross. The Holy Spirit reveals these truths to us as we mature in the faith and as we continue in worship, prayer, and reading.

Power in Jesus' Name

There is power in the name of Jesus, and the early disciples knew this in their ministry of healing. We should take courage, and learn to say His name in personal worship, and thus make His Person an intimate part of our lives. After that, having a prayer-partner seems right and good. And after that we find it easier to share our faith (the word *evangelism* seems such an impossible thing for many people) because what we are doing is speaking of the One we love the most and sharing that love.

> Hitherto you have asked nothing in my name; ask, and you will receive, that your joy may be full (John 16:24).

My prayer:

> Lord Jesus, help me to memorize words which give You praise, and use them until they become my own. Then teach me, out of the fullness of my heart, to express my own praise from my spirit and from my heart. Amen.

Keep Close to Jesus

> I am the light of the world;
> he who follows me
> will not walk in darkness,

but will have the
light of life (John 8:12).

How does one have light for all the decisions
of life? By keeping close to Jesus. How do we
stay close to anyone? By being with him, by
getting to know him. I heard a story once
about a Jewish rabbi whose student boasted
that he really had come to know his teacher.

Rabbi: Do you know what I like?
       Do you know what is important to me?
       Do you know where I hurt?
       . . . then you don't know *me*.

Youth is forever dreaming of and looking for
such a person—one who gives mutual trust
and confidence. As the years go by we are dis-
illusioned, whether we admit it or not, by our
inability to trust, to love, and to forgive. We
humans seem to have a conspiracy not to be
honest with each other—to hide our hurts. It's
called "etiquette." When a mutually trusting
human relationship is found, or when I observe one, I feel grateful to God, but there is a
price for such a oneness.

There is only one cure that I know of for that
inner aloneness or loneliness. Loneliness in the
U.S.A. reaches such gigantic proportions that
it has become like a disease.

The only effective remedy is to keep close to
Jesus, like the branch lives in the vine. Jesus
promised this oneness and satisfaction to that
woman of dubious character in Samaria.

A fountain of living water
right in her heart.

The fountain of God's unconditional
love which is satisfying.
The fountain which quenches
all inner thirsts (John 4).

This fountain makes it unnecessary to be continually seeking or pulling upon another person for an impossible fulfillment.

This promise was a lifesaver for me on my first furlough from China, when I was faced with the fragility of human love and found the verse, "Whosoever drinks of the water I shall give him shall never thirst." Shall means shall. Never means never. Thirst means any unsatisfied need.

Jesus became more dear and near, and the Bible became more understandable and spoke to me. Jesus became my Rock, my strong tower, my deliverer, my fortress, and my very reason for living. I love hymns about Jesus, like the meditation at the beginning of this chapter.

The very first verse I ever memorized in the Chinese language was Acts 4:12, and I still repeat it often in the midst of my praise to Him:

There is salvation in no one else, for
there is no other name under heaven
given among men by which we must
be saved.

Union with Christ

In one of my creative meditations on the Vine of John 15, I ask you to close your eyes and imagine you are a branch growing out of that Vine, Christ Jesus. Then look up and look down. See other branches like you, and unlike you, who are also Christ's. Give thanks for them.

In my workshops I am brought into close contact with churches of all denominations, and I am seeing the love which is blossoming between Protestants and Roman Catholics who love Jesus. We are all on one Vine. My dear mother, now in heaven, must know all this and rejoice.

Can anything be closer than the way a branch is joined to the Vine? John 15 is one of my favorite chapters, and John 17 comes next, because there Jesus is praying that complete union might exist:

> I in them and thou in me . . .
> that the love which thou [Father]
> hast for me, may be in them
> and I in them.

All of my prayers will never be answered (and I'm glad), nor will all of yours, because we do not always rightly discern the will of God. But one thing I know for sure: Every prayer that Jesus Christ prayed on earth for us will be answered. He knew that His body, the visible church, would be divided and fractured, yet He prayed:

> I pray for . . . those who are to believe
> in me through their word,
> that they may all be one,
> even as thou, Father, art in me,

and I in thee, that they may
also be in us, so that the world
may believe that thou hast sent me.

—John 17:20,21

Aids to Heart-Worship and Meditation

In this last portion of my book, I am sharing with you some of the precious material which has come to mean so much to me during the last 15 years.

The Jesus Prayer is one which I teach in my workshops. The rest are items from liturgical services or prayer books, which have been like launching pads to send my spirit into praise and adoration and sometimes intercession.

I copy them, put them in my purse, memorize them, and pray them. Give careful attention to the words and meaning, and your heart will soon be full of joy and praise. I find that I express my love by the use of the names of God in meditation and in prayer.

It is difficult for me to select one and say that it is my favorite. I love to pray the Confession, for it humbles me. I need the Collect for Grace and the Daily Prayer. The Priestly Song makes me lose track of time, as I relish those phrases over and over in worship. To adore my Lord, there is nothing like the Gloria. The Nicene Creed and Mary's Canticle are also my favorites.

I hope those I have included will come to be meaningful in your life too.

Oh, how I love thy law!
  It is my meditation
  all the day.
Your commandment makes me wiser
  than my enemies,
  for it is ever with me.
I have more understanding
  than all my teachers,
  for thy testimonies are
  my meditation.
I understand more than the aged,
  for I keep thy precepts. . . .
How sweet are thy words
  to my taste,
  sweeter than honey
  to my mouth!

Psalm 119:97-103

Meditation is the art of slowly turning a phrase over and over in one's mind until it gets into one's heart. We don't do much of that kind of reading today. Meditation is waiting, listening, and repeating a phrase or one of the names of the Lord Jesus in the quietness of our hearts.

The Jesus Prayer

The short and simple prayer known as the Jesus Prayer came down to us from the early Christians, and for centuries was lost to the Western world. I first heard of it through a leaflet published by The Forward Movement (Episcopal Church) and since have read George

A. Maloney, S.J., *The Prayer of the Heart,* Chapter 6, and Morton T. Kelsey, Ph.D., *The Other Side of Silence,* Chapter 11.

It is adapted from the prayer of blind Bartimaeus:

> Lord Jesus Christ, Son of God,
> have mercy on me, a sinner.

The very simplicity of this prayer is deceptive, yet its benefits are far-reaching for the one who is hungry and thirsty for a closer walk with the Lord. It is a way of listening. It is a technique. It keeps the mind free from dreaming. It is a protection from assaults of the enemy. It leads to greater love of Jesus.

After reading the two authors mentioned above, I took their suggestions to combine deep breathing with the repetition of that prayer. Their predictions were true. My spirit was quieted at once, any turmoil of mind or emotions was also quieted, and my body began to relax. The presence of Jesus with and within me was fulfilling and healing.

I started using the words they gave me, and soon I was adding or substituting other words as my heart found them there. I'll illustrate.

Lord Jesus Christ	Jesus, Lord . . .
	Christ Jesus my Lord . . .
	Jesus, Jesus . . .
Son of God	Son of the living God . . .
	Beloved Son of God . . .
Have mercy on me	Lord, have mercy . . .
	Christ, have mercy . . .
A sinner	A miserable sinner . . .

An undeserving sinner . . .
A forgiven sinner . . .

The variations: Your heart will tell you, as mine does, for I recognize Jesus Christ as my Lord, my Saviour, my Master. And I recognize myself as a sinner—past, present, future, being saved from life's pressures, stresses, and hurts.

The position of the body doesn't matter as long as I am relaxing. Some instructions tell you to sit, others to lie down. I practice this in conjunction with the slow, rhythmic strokes I use when I swim, as well as when I can't sleep, or when I am driving.

Breathe in slowly and deeply, and say:
    Lord Jesus Christ . . . (wait)
Breathe out slowly, and say:
    Son of God . . . (wait)
Breathe in slowly:
    have mercy on me . . . (wait)
Breathe out slowly:
    a sinner.

Sometimes after working for hours at my desk, when I stretch out slowly to rest, I start the deep breathing and use my fingers to count, slowly putting slight pressure on the tip of each, until I've said the prayer 10 times, 20 times, or more.

This brings Jesus very near to me, and the breathing helps my body recover from the fatigue of writing. I am bound afresh to Him by the repetition of His Name.

How sweet the Name of Jesus sounds
In a believer's ear!

It soothes his sorrows, heals his
   wounds,
And drives away his fear.

A few of my favorite meditations:

A Collect for Grace

Lord God, almighty and everlasting
Father, you have brought us in safety to
this new day: Preserve us with your
mighty power, that we may not fall into
sin, nor be overcome by adversity; and in
all we do, direct us to the fulfilling of your
purpose: through Jesus Christ our Lord.
Amen.

—Book of Common Prayer, p. 100.

My Daily Prayer

Father, you are filled with life and power
   while we are weak and in need.
We beg you now and every day
   to fracture the power of sin in our lives
   and to flood us with the light of your
   love who is Jesus Christ,
   who lives and rules with you and the
   Holy Spirit, one God, now and forever.
   Amen.

—Breviary, p. 334.

The Confession of Sins

Most merciful God,
I confess that I have sinned against you
in thought, word and deed,
by what I have done,
and by what I have left undone.

I have not loved you with
   my whole heart
I have not loved my neighbors
   as myself.
I am truly sorry and I humbly repent.
For the sake of your Son Jesus Christ,
have mercy on me and forgive me,
that I may delight in your will
and walk in your ways,
to the glory of your Name. Amen.

—Book of Common Prayer, p. 360.

Song: Priestly People

Priestly people, Kingly people,
Holy People, God's chosen people,
Sing praise to the Lord.

We sing praise to you, O Christ,
   beloved Son of the Father.
We give you praise, O Wisdom
   everlasting, O Word of God.

We sing to you, O Son, born of
   Mary the Virgin.
We give you praise, our Brother,
   born to heal us, our saving Lord.

We sing to you, O brightness of
   splendor and glory.
We sing to you, O Morning Star,
   announcing the coming day.

We sing to you, O light bringing men
   out of darkness,

We give you praise, O guiding Light,
who shows us the way to heaven.

—Lucien Deiss (PMB-141)[1]

(This is one of my favorites, giving praise to
Christ.)

The Gloria

Glory to God in the highest,
and peace to his people on earth.

Lord God, heavenly King,
almighty God and Father,
we worship you, we give you thanks,
we praise you for your glory.

Lord Jesus Christ, only Son of the Father,
Lord God, Lamb of God,
you take away the sin of the world;
have mercy on us;
you are seated at the right hand of the
Father: receive our prayer.

For you alone are the Holy One,
you alone are the Lord,
you alone are the Most High,
Jesus Christ,
with the Holy Spirit,
in the glory of God the Father. Amen.

—Book of Common Prayer, p. 356
Holy Eucharist II

---

[1]American Interim Breviary, Prayer of Christians.
Catholic Book Publishing Co., N.Y., © 1971, p. 718.

Praise be to thee, O Christ

His name . . . is powerful.
His name . . . is wonderful.
His name . . . is healing.
Let us use His name boldly.
Let us say it aloud, and not
    whisper it timidly.
Let us say it with faith,
    with hope, with love.

Let us sing together:

All pow'r is given in Jesus' name
    in earth and heaven, in Jesus' name,
And in Jesus' name I come to you
    to share His power as He told me to:

The peace of God, which passeth all
    understanding,
  keep your hearts and minds in
  the knowledge and love of God,
  and of his Son Jesus Christ our Lord;
And the blessing of God Almighty,
  the Father, the Son, and the Holy Ghost,
  be amongst you, and remain with you
    always.

                              Amen.

Meditation for Chapter 12

Jesus, I am resting, resting
   In the joy of what Thou art;
I am finding out the greatness
   Of Thy loving heart.
Thou hast bid me gaze upon Thee,
   And Thy beauty fills my soul,
For by Thy transforming power,
   Thou hast made me whole.

Simply trusting Thee, Lord Jesus,
   I behold Thee as Thou art,
And Thy love, so pure, so changeless,
   Satisfies my heart;
Satisfies its deepest longings,
   Meets, supplies its every need,
Compasseth me round with blessings;
   Thine is love indeed!

—Jean S. Pigott

CHAPTER 12

Books Which Have Helped Me

Chapter 1—Stop Trying So Hard!
Chapter 2—You Can Know Who You Are

1. *Love Yourself,* by Walter Trobisch (Inter-Varsity Press, Downers Grove, Illinois 60515, © 1976). Paper, 54 pp.
Author: Walter Trobisch is known worldwide as a counselor, lecturer, and writer of books on love—God's love and human love.
Comment: A warm, personal, and practical book. Good illustrations about people like yourself.
Contents: Themes on self-love versus self-hate, self-acceptance versus self-rejection, the joy of living versus the depths of depression.

2. *Beginning to Pray,* by Anthony Bloom (Paulist Press, Paramus, New Jersey 07652, © 1970). Paper, 75 pp.
Author: A Russian Orthodox Archbishop (England and Ireland). Once a French resistance fighter and army surgeon. One of the great spiritual masters.
Contents: A classic on simplicity and understanding why God is sometimes absent. How to address Him. How to manage time.
Quote: "We cannot live a life of prayer, we cannot go ahead Godwards, unless we are

free from possession in order to have two hands to offer and a heart absolutely open . . . and an intelligence completely open, to the unknown and the unexpected. This is the way in which we are rich and yet totally free from richness."

3. *Better Health and Miracle Living,* by Oral Roberts (Oral Roberts Evangelistic Association, Tulsa, Oklahoma, © 1976). Paper, 299 pp.

Author: World-known evangelist, healer, and author. Founder of Oral Roberts University and City of Faith Hospital.

Comments: Practical, easily read. Big print. A healing can be a matter of weeks or months with medical assistance and prayer. A miracle is an instant healing. Full of affirmations and steps to physical and spiritual healing.

Contents: Three steps: Have a right relationship with God, plant good seed with people you like or dislike, and have a right relationship with yourself.

4. *God Loves You,* by Rosalind Rinker (Two cassettes in book form. Order from Rosalind Rinker, 2400/3A via Mariposa West, Laguna Hills, California 92653).

Comment: Used by a man and his wife caring for disturbed children "because the very tone of your voice brought quietness to the children and assurance to us."

Contents: Three messages: God loves you, God is always near you, God wants to help you.

His intentions toward us are everlasting love that is not based on our deserving. Messages are faith-builders.

Chapter 4—How to Practice the Presence of God

1. *Nesting in the Rock,* by George A. Maloney, S.J. (Dimension Books, Denville, New Jersey 07834, © 1977). Paper, 167 pp.

Author and Comment: One of my favorite authors and in-depth teachers on prayer and contemplation. A prolific writer who speaks under inspiration and with authority.

Contents: Finding the Father in all events, abandonment to God's dynamic love, abandonment to human love, abandonment in contemplation, etc.

Chapter 5—Why the Deity of Our Lord Is Important

1. *The Trinity,* by Robert Crossley (InterVarsity Press, Downers Grove, Illinois 60515, © 1965). Paper, 43 pp.

Author: Robert Crossley is chaplain of Ridley Hall, Cambridge University, England.

Contents: One of the clearest booklets I've seen on the similar attributes of the Father, Son, and Holy Spirit, and the differing ministries of each. I buy this in quantities to be available in my workshops.

Chapter 6—Obedience to the Holy Spirit

1. *Nine Sweet Fruits*, by Mary Lee Ehrlich (Tyndale House, Wheaton, Illinois 60187, © 1981). Paper, 154 pp.

Author: Homemaker, author, and Bible teacher of women's classes.

Comments: Nineteen years ago Mary Lee read my book *Prayer-Conversing With God*, and with four women began to pray faith-sized requests. They were amazed at the answers. Thus her teaching/writing career began.

Contents: Nine chapters on the fruits of the Spirit. Fascinating reading with lists of practical things which women love. Filled with personal and family illustrations for implementing the power Christ has promised us through His Holy Spirit.

2 . *Fasting Rediscovered*, by Thomas Ryan (Paulist Press, 545 Island Road, Ramsey, New Jersey 07446, © 1981). Paper, 160 pp.

Author: Fr. Thomas Ryan is a Paulist priest who has worked as a chaplain in campus ministry at Ohio State and McGill Universities. At present he is engaged in studies in Switzerland and France.

Comments: The first book I've found which looks at fasting as more than abstinence from food, and instructs in the preparation of one's mind and spirit through God's help.

Contents: Fasting is worship, ministry, an act of religious joy, an act of faith, hope, and love; prayer and meditation; leads to deeper union with God; is restful and helps us to celebrate.

Chapter 7—The Sin Which Blocks Prayer

1 . *Guilt and Grace,* by Paul Tournier (Harper & Row, New York, © 1962). 224 pp.

Author: Swiss psychiatrist and prolific author on books relating psychology to Christian practice and belief.

Comment: Reading Dr. Tournier's *The Meaning of Persons* was a turning point in my walk with God. I began to accept my liabilities in the same spirit as my assets.

Contents: Dr. Tournier probes behind our daily irritability, our aggressiveness and indifference. He exposes the hidden sources that give rise to guilt, conflict, repression, responsibility, choice, confession, license, and freedom.

2. *Healing Life's Hurts,* by Dennis Linn, S.J., and Matthew Linn, S.J. (Paulist Press, Ramsey, New Jersey 07446, © 1978). Paper, 246 pp.

Authors: Two young priests whose ministry among the Sioux of South Dakota was so anointed by God that they are now free for world ministry.

Comment: I've attended one of their all-day workshops. They are delightfully refreshing and Christ-centered, with audience participation.

Contents: Healing Memories Through the Five

Steps of Forgiveness.
Part I. What Happens in Healing a Memory.
Part II. Emotional and Physical Healing.
Part III. Predispositions for Five Stages of Dying and Forgiveness.
Part IV. Five Stages of Dying and Forgiveness.
Part V. Eucharist—Summary of Five Steps of Dying and Forgiveness.
Part VI. Getting Started on Healing a Memory.
Appendix: Prayers, Affirmations, and Other Helps.
Excellent charts pinpointing areas of need and steps of wholeness.

3. *The Key to Everything,* by Norman Grubb (Union Life Ministries, 656 Taft Avenue, Glen Ellyn, Illinois 60137). Leaflet.
Author: Prolific author of books on spiritual growth and personal holiness.
Comments: I purchase this little handbook in quantities of 50 and always have one to give away to someone who is looking for God's secret of sustained freedom from guilt.
Contents: Unbelievable simplicity in the truth of what to ask for, how to receive, and how to be a container for Christ's presence.

Chapter 8—How Our Spiritual Lives Are Affected by Stress

1. *None of These Diseases,* by S. I. McMillen, M.D. (Spire Books, F. H. Revell & Co., Old

Tappan, New Jersey, © 1963). Paper, 158 pp.

Author: A born-again M.D. who states that this book contains prescriptions which thousands of his patients needed but at the time only received inadequate help.

Comment: A Christian classic on the freedom from disease which modern medicine cannot duplicate. Everyone should read this. A book you cannot put down.

Contents: Revealing chapters prescribed for the millions who generate their own disease by damaging life habits . . . on the most prevalent diseases of modern man. Full of illustrations.

2. *Your Churning Place*, by Robert L. Wise (Regal Books, Division G/L Publications, Glendale, California 91209, © 1977). Paper, 142 pp.

Author: Pastor, counselor, author.

Comment: I've spoken twice in his church in Oklahoma City. Robert Wise is a man with a great heart and a great message, pastoring a fast-growing congregation.

Contents: An enlightening and practical book which pinpoints where your emotions affect some part of your body. Turns stress into strength as you learn to cope. You can know the wholeness of Christ. Chapters on:

Guilt the Avenger.
Self-Centeredness—the Ego and I.
Escapism—Checking Out.
Change—The Hooded Bandit.

Jealousy—The Green-Eyed Monster.
Anxiety—The Gnawing Devourer.

3. *Anatomy of an Illness*, by Norman Cousins (W.W. Norton & Co., © 1979; Bantam Books, Inc.). 173 pp.

Author: Former editor of *Saturday Review* and a well-known cultural statesman.

Contents: A successful fight against a crippling disease. This story has been told in major medical journals around the world. The doctor helped the patient use his own powers, which were laughter, courage, and tenacity to mobilize his body's natural healing resources. A striking example of what the mind and body working together can do to overcome illness.

4. *90 Days to Self-Health*, by C. Norman Shealy, M.D. (Dial Press, New York 10017, © 1977; Bantam Books). Paper, 204 pp.

Author: Dr. Shealy is a neurosurgeon and a pioneer of the holistic health movement, as well as the Director of the Pain Rehabilitation Center in Wisconsin.

Comment: A sound psychological approach to mental and physical health. Very helpful to the uninitiated. I am using it for relaxation exercises.

Contents: Ninety-day program. Nutrition, relaxation, affirmations, guided exercises, biogenics, causes of pain.

**Chapter 9— Benefits of
a Prayer Partner
Chapter 10—The Prayer of Faith-Sized
Requests**

1. *As Bread That Is Broken,* by Peter G. van Breemen, S.J. (Dimension Books, Denville, New Jersey 07834, © 1974). Paper, 187 pp.

Author: Fr. Breemen has his Ph.D. in atomic physics. He is a Dutch Jesuit and a man of deep prayer. His writing has the eternal freshness of the daily bread of the Eucharist. He writes in depth with bold simplicity.

Comment: For two years I carried this book with me on all my travels to speaking engagements, and I gave many copies away. I recommend it highly if you are looking for in-depth teaching on God's love and prayer.

Contents: Twenty chapters on how we (like bread) are consumed in the gift of ourselves to our fellow men and women. We die in order to rise to new life.

2. *Healing Through Prayer,* by Francis Mac-Nutt, Ph.D., O.P. (Ave Maria Press, Notre Dame, Indiana 46556, © 1974; Bantam Books). Paper, 86 pp.

Author: One of the first priests to be involved in the Catholic charismatic renewal. Active in healing ministry for more than 15 years. Started with Mrs. Agnes Sanford.

Comment: A small abridged booklet condensed from his first book, *Healing.* A handbook everyone should own.

Contents: Four basic kinds of healing, including healing of memories. Discovering the healing power of Christ over physical, emotional, and spiritual ills through the gift of the Holy Spirit.

3. *The Power to Heal*, by Francis MacNutt, Ph.D., O.P. (Ave Maria Press, Notre Dame, Indiana 46556, © 1977). Paper, 254 pp.

Author: Same as above.

Comment: Sequel to his first book, *Healing*, with deepened understanding. Faith-building illustrations.

Contents: New insights into healing: soaking prayer, the time element, the wounded healed, suffering and death, and others.

4. *Healing Prayer*, by William Portsmouth (Arthur James, Ltd., The Drift, Evesham, Worcester, England, © 1954). 10 editions, 156 pp.

Author: Rev. William Portsmouth, the Bishop of Worcester.

Comment: My copy is well-marked and beloved.

Contents: Prepared for use by the sick and those who minister to them at home or in the hospital. Chapters on praying for health, the healing God, health within, the disease consciousness, the healthy attitude, meditation and how to use it. Morning and evening readings of affirmative healing prayer, with carefully chosen prayers for one month.

5. *Prayer—An Exciting Adventure*, by Reginald Goff (Prayer Unlimited, 1621 Andros Place, Tucson, Arizona 85705, 101 pp.).
Author: Reginald Goff, a pastor of the United Methodist Church, and author of two books. Together with his wife, Verla, they are world travelers and speakers for Camp Farthest Out, and personal friends of mine.
Comment and Contents: This is the story of answered prayer. In a small Wyoming town, four women started to pray for key men in their church, and renewal began until there were 17 prayer groups. The membership grew from 285 to 1000 in a town of less than 5000, with 16 other churches. A half-city block contained the new church and educational buildings; 20 young people went into Christian service where there had not been one in 50 years! Even the police force and other city offices were cleaned up.
6 . *Helps to Answered Prayer*, Reginald Goff's second book.

Chapter 11—The Prayers of Meditation and Worship

1. *Living Prayer*, by Anthony Bloom (Darton, Longman & Todd, Ltd., England, © 1966; published in the U.S.A. by Templegate Publishers, Springfield, Illinois 62705). Paper, 125 pp.
Author: See Chapter 1, *Beginning to Pray*.
Comment: Refreshing and thought-provoking.
Contents: Some chapter headings; The Lord's

Prayer, The Prayer of Bartimaeus and the Jesus Prayer, Unanswered Prayer and Petition, The Prayer of Silence.

Quote: "More than any other prayer, the Jesus Prayer aims at bringing us to stand in God's presence with no other thought but the miracle of our standing there and God with us, because in the use of the Jesus Prayer there is nothing and no one except God and us" (p. 88).

2. *The Other Side of Silence*, by Morton T. Kelsey, Ph.D. (Paulist Press, Paramus, New Jersey 07652, © 1976). Paper, 314 pp.

Author: Dr. Kelsey is an Episcopal Ph.D. teaching in Notre Dame, a Catholic University. A prolific writer of books and pamphlets, he thoroughly researches any subject he writes or speaks about. A book laymen will find inspirational and informative.

Comment: One of my favorite books, which God has used to give me guidance and wisdom to know His will in making difficult decisions.

Contents: A classic on meditation—its history, its need, and various ways to practice this discipline. Half the book is on visualization, use of imagination, and meditations from the Gospels, poems, allegories, etc., plus the art of making positive affirmations.

3. *Inward Stillness*, by George A. Maloney, S.J. (Dimension Books, Inc., Denville, New Jersey 07834, © 1976). Paper, 228 pp.

Author: Same as *Nesting in the Rock* (Chapter 4).

Comment: Being a writer myself, when I find an author who goes deeper than I have yet gone, I am refreshed, fed, and strengthened. Fr. Maloney's books do this for me. I recommend them.

Contents: An invitation to accept God's call, "Be still and know that I am God" (Psalm 46:10). Chapters include: The Silence of God, Praying in the Heart (Jesus Prayer), Jesus Christ—Lord of my Unconscious, Prayer as Healing, etc.

4. *Using The Jesus Prayer*, by Bede Thomas Mudge, O.H.C. (Leaflet. The Forward Movement Publications, 412 Sycamore Street, Cincinnati, Ohio 45202).

5. *A Simple Way to Meditate*, by Jim Scully (Leaflet showing how to use the Jesus Prayer. Dove Publications, Pecos, New Mexico 87552).

Meditation for Chapter 13

May the mind of Christ my Saviour
  Live in me from day to day,
By His love and power controlling
  All I do and say.

May the Word of God dwell richly
  In my heart from hour to hour,
So that all may see I triumph
  Only through His power.

May the peace of God my Father
  Rule my life in everything,
That I may be calm to comfort
  Sick and sorrowing.

May the love of Jesus fill me,
  As the waters fill the sea;
Him exalting, self abasing—
  This is victory.

May His beauty rest upon me
  As I seek the lost to win,
And may they forget the channel,
  Seeing only Him.

                    —Kate B. Wilkinson

CHAPTER 13

Inspirational Summary

This book can be used in a series of lessons, and the last session could be a helpful review of how each member has profited. The combined sharing will bring to mind afresh many of the things we want to remember.

Suggestion: Each member select one chapter and bring something to class to share, either to read from a marked portion or to tell how it has personally enriched his or her life.

Chapter 1: Stop Trying So Hard!

Becoming a child in Jesus' arms. Being free to talk with Him and accept His love. Affirmations of love. Six points to help start a Quiet Time.

Chapter 2: You Can Know Who You Are

The difference between relationship and fellowship. Accepting the negatives of life and turning them to positives. Sharing God's love.

Chapter 3: How to Pray-Read Your Bible

Six different ways to read your Bible. How God speaks to us. The value of owning several Bible translations.

Chapter 4: How to Practice the Presence of God

Enriching your life by knowing how to use your time. A lifetime habit to be cultivated. Finding other books on this subject.

Chapter 5: Why the Deity of Our Lord Is Important

The three claims Jesus made for Himself, and where they may be found. The importance of this truth in the development of one's personal life and ministry. ("Ministry" means sharing our faith with others.)

Chapter 6: Obedience to the Holy Spirit

Three tests for guidance. Three things that hinder the Spirit. Ways to determine God's best from our idea of what is good. Eleven ways the Holy Spirit helps us when we pray.

Chapter 7: The Sin Which Blocks Prayer

Jesus names the sin which blocks prayer. Bible references to note and mark. The dynamics of confession. Healing of memories. Benefits of a spiritual advisor. Visualization in prayer.

Chapter 8: How Our Spiritual Lives Are Affected by Stress

Common symptoms, ailments, and emotions which distress us. God's program for health. Five illustrations and what each person learned about himself/herself. Jesus' knowledge of the human mind. How to handle stress successfully. Practical ways we can promote our own health.

Chapter 9: The Benefits of a Prayer Partner

Finding a prayer-partner. Benefits. Fears of praying aloud. First lessons in prayer. Special promises. Ros shares her experiences with a Friday morning group.

Chapter 10: The Prayer of Faith-Sized Requests

Visualize your answer. Praying in the will of God. The prayer of faith: Denise's healing. Five questions people always ask. The prayer of binding and loosing: the story of Crying Wind. Eight things we learn about the prayer of faith.

Chapter 11: The Prayers of Meditation and Worship

The precious name of Jesus and its power. Keeping close to Jesus: the vine and the branch, and union with Him. Ros shares her experience. The Jesus Prayer—benefits and directions for breathing with variations. Some of Ros's favorite portions of the liturgy as found in the Book of Common Prayer.

Chapter 12: Books Which Have Helped Me

This is my bibliography. Many books are listed under chapter headings, with a brief sentence reviewing the contents, in order to make it easier for you to select the one you would like to read.

Chapter 13: Inspirational Summary

of the contents of each chapter. A practical and inspirational aid for review and for remembering.

Thank you, my friends, and God's Peace be with you.

Rosalind Rinker
2400/3A Mariposa West
Laguna Hills, CA 92653

May
the Power
of the Father,
the Love
of the Son,
and the Wisdom
of the Holy Ghost
guard,
hold,
and guide
you forever.

~Amen

K. Forkish